Speaking Frankly About

Customer

Relationship

Management

J.C. QUINTANA

To

My wife Shelley...

Thank you for your amazing support.

My kids Reina, Nathaniel, Jonathan, Michael, and Adriana ... You inspire me to write.

My grandkids Breanna and Alex...

You make me proud every day.

Printed in the United States of America.

Speaking Frankly About Customer Relationship Management

Copyright © JC Quintana

www.CRGPress.com

CRG Press and Corporate Relationship Group®

Kennesaw, Georgia. United States

ISBN 978-0-9889145-3-7 (Hardback)

Third Edition 2014

CONTENTS

FOREWORD
BY DR DAN DANA

"All sales are relationship sales." This pearl of wisdom has long been known and intuitively understood by successful sales people. That is, the features and benefits (and price) of a company's products are less important than the relationship the prospective customer/client has with the company, and especially with individuals ("real people") who represent the company. The primacy of relationship over attributes of offered products and services occurs even in "virtual" enterprises in which clients and customers may never even meet, see, or speak to a "real person" in the company, ever more common in our internet age. A relationship nevertheless exists, and its quality is of vital importance to the enterprise's commercial success.

Herein, JC Quintana extends this principle more broadly to include all relationships that constitute a corporation's presence in the minds of everyone who experiences interactions with it and its representatives, internally and externally. (It's worth noting that his affectionate dedication to his children and wife in the front matter of this volume indicates that JC "walks the talk" in his personal, as well as his professional, life. The dedication oozes respect and mutual trust, the essential "stuff" of successful relationships in any sector of life.)

Readers will recognize the depth and breadth of JC's knowledge and intuitive understanding of corporate relationship management, drawn from his extensive career experience in the real world of business. His professional success in the CRM industry testifies to his qualifications for writing this book, a vehicle for sharing his wisdom with others.

Dr. Dan Dana, Ph.D.

Educator and author in the field of workplace conflict management and mediation and Founder of the Mediation Training Institute International.

FOREWORD
BY JOHN MARCHICA

Several years ago, around the time when some people fretted over Y2K, I realized that my coveted method of keeping track of Very Important People had to go. Yes, I was proud of the cascading list of names, neatly nested within columns and rows on my spreadsheet. Names with color-coded priorities assigned to them, telling me what I needed to do. Many were blue (it's cool, no need to worry). Others were shouting at me in bold red (do something!) My favorites were green: paying clients.

I had done very well with my lists until the day someone introduced me to the concept of CRM. It was the early days of these nascent technologies, and companies like mine began to experiment with CRM tools. As I began to use my first CRM software I remember at first being intimidated by its complexity. But I soon became so enamored by its organizational power that I forgot the reason it had been suggested to me in the first place. I now had a bigger and better toolkit, and I was playing with my tools. My first attempt at CRM was what one would call a Failed Implementation.

This book makes the seemingly straightforward argument that CRM is about relationships and the value that you place on them. In the traditional sense, CRM is very much like a better mousetrap than my color-coded spreadsheets: all about the customer (the first C in CRM) and improving how you manage that relationship.

You may have guessed that the person who introduced me to CRM was JC Quintana. JC understands that people like me—traditional users of CRM software—have a narrower view about what CRM is and what it can do. To many of us CRM is a means to keeping track of people, typically defined as customers and prospects. But that is a very limited interpretation of the value of CRM.

In JC's world, those "people" extend beyond customers and prospects to employees, vendors, suppliers, and others. All the stakeholders in the system are connected in one way or another. Consequently, a truly empowered CRM vision, fully embraced by an organization, can lead to more profound connections among all stakeholders. A robust CRM system is designed help a company be better equipped to fulfill the needs of everyone involved, from client to coworker. When everyone is a part of the solution, the level of commitment by everyone is strengthened across the organization.

This worldview is less transactional than the common take on CRM; instead, it underlies a holistic approach to how a company should operate. In my view, this framework leads to better decision-making by everyone involved. Customers are better informed about what they're buying and with whom they are dealing. Employees have an intrinsic interest in meeting their commitments to both customers and their peers. A holistic approach to CRM has built-in accountability at all levels. The result: a shared sense of purpose and increased levels of trust among all stakeholders.

About a decade ago, when JC and I worked together, I was steadfastly studying and writing about the idea of accountability in the workplace. Following the collapse of Arthur Andersen, Enron, WorldCom and others, people were calling for better accountability from corporate America—the end result being the infamous Sarbanes-Oxley Act of 2002 that set new standards and enforcement for publicly traded companies and public accounting firms. The goal of the legislation, in part, was to restore trust in American business.

Five years after its implementation, our economic system was on the verge of collapse by another group of bad actors in the commercial banking and investments sector. The Dodd-Frank Wall Street and Consumer Protection Act was the response, imposing new rules and regulations on the financial services industry and the regulatory agencies responsible for oversight. Again, the goal was to provide a framework to restore trust and accountability in these institutions.

In a way, a good CRM system functions like Sarbanes-Oxley and Dodd-Frank, but without the punitive intent. It works in the background helping people play by a set of rules that produces a better outcome. Soon, stakeholders make decisions with better information and begin to work collaboratively. Increased accountability and trust are byproducts of the system. If you want to understand why this happens, and more importantly how to build the foundation for such a system, this book is for you.

When I first met JC we had lofty goals about how businesses should be run. We would talk for hours about the company I had and the new company that we were building. We used weighty words like integrity and accountability. We considered our purpose in business and in life and where the two traversed. But we also believed that work should be fun, that work should bring joy to our lives and the others around us. I still feel that way, and JC does too.

If you are lucky enough to meet JC one day, you'll see that he is often beaming from ear to ear. You will be struck by his joyful presence. You will know that he cares. I know that this book has been a labor of love—his passion leaps off the page and demands your attention.

This book is an expression of his optimism, a call-to-action for companies not to be great, but to be exceptional. I welcome you to actualize JC's vision, set forth on these pages, within your organization and beyond.

John Marchica

Author of *The Accountable Organization*

ABOUT THE AUTHOR

JC Quintana, christened the "Servant of the People" by his clients for his passion for service, is a fervid thought leader and innovator of corporate relationship and customer experience management strategies and technology.

Over the past twenty years, JC's celebrated career has included leadership roles for consulting firms and CRM technology companies in the United States, Asia, Europe, and Latin America. His distinctive combination of skills gives JC a fresh and empathetic perspective that he shares in his books and at leadership conferences throughout the globe.

JC currently serves as the worldwide Chief Innovation Executive for Customer Experience Management for one of the world's most-respected technology companies. A proud father of five and grandfather of two, JC lives in Kennesaw, Georgia with his wife Shelley.

INTRODUCTION:
SPEAKING FRANKLY

I wanted to start this book by telling you how skilled I am at the strategies and technologies we associate with Customer Relationship Management or CRM. In a series of well-positioned statements, I had planned to impress you with my years of experience as a CRM consultant and technologist. My masterfully crafted resume would include an illustrious history in "key" roles at the top CRM technology companies in the world, followed by a few names of people you may or may not know who have "fathered" this industry and shaped the practices that have "catalyst" the success of initiatives all over the globe.

However, I cannot be so arrogant as to assign myself a "key" role within an ever-growing effort that has so intimately changed the way we perceive customers and our need to become grateful servants to each. Nor can I baptize any one person as having "fathered" a concept so aligned with our human needs and depth of connection and purpose. And, I certainly do not know exactly how one catalyzes inanimate business objects in any direction.

What I am, and have been for more than twenty years, is an advocate. An advocate of people and the idea that, to be successful, we have to speak frankly about the strategies that build relationships with other people in business. What I rather do in this book is speak to you transparently about the steps it takes to gather people in your company around the topic of customer relationship and customer experience management and the collaborations, interactions, relationships and conversations you must have to be successful. I emphasize the word "conversations" because, in spite of the vast resources available about CRM, there is yet to be a resource that helps us initiate frank conversations together, across the company, on this topic.

Speaking frankly and challenging the status quo is a difficult part of launching any initiative, but in particular, initiatives like CRM that aim to build relationships with customers through the unilateral support of all leaders and employees within the company. It is an already challenging task to gain consensus and support from the people heading the sales, marketing, and support organizations of your company. But failing to engage in in-depth conversations about expectations is where CRM initiatives actually fail.

This book is divided into ten sections, each representing a critical topic of conversation in which everyone in your company must engage relating to customer relationship management:

ARTICLE 1: INTRO TO A MANIFESTO

Written as a "call to arms" to every person, at every level within your organization, it encourages conversation about your goals for CRM and how they will impact the people who are charged with making it successful. It is an invitation to set clear expectations and to make CRM the vehicle that connects all your corporate teams with the vision of improving the central relationships of your business through interactions that are meaningful and intentional.

ARTICLE 2: POWER TO THE ACRONYM

Submits that CRM is exactly that, Customer Relationship Management. In spite of the bad reputation that has marred the acronym, CRM works. This section encourages conversations about what CRM means or will mean to your company and motivates you to focus on your individual objectives and goals by looking across the entire business. It also connects the vision of managing customer relationships and customer experiences as a joint and complementary strategy.

ARTICLE 3: POWER TO THE COLLABORATION

Calls for each member of your organization to work together to assess customer relationship management initiatives and implement them successfully, together. It encourages conversations about the level of collaboration you will need and the barriers you need to overcome.

ARTICLE 4: POWER TO THE RESOLUTION

Explores the important questions people are asking about CRM and guides you through the best ways to answer them to ensure company-wide support. It encourages transparent, open conversations about the topics people need to understand, and the expectations they need to clarify, in order to engage wholeheartedly.

ARTICLE 5: POWER TO THE RELATIONSHIPS

Expands on the similarities between personal and business relationships and expounds on how CRM can be the right strategy to help building them. It encourages conversations about the business relationships you are trying to cultivate and how you are either nurturing them or neglecting them.

ARTICLE 6: POWER TO THE INTERACTION

Brings awareness to particular, critical interactions your company must manage for genuine, heart-felt service to result. This section encourages conversations about the specific things we do, or not do, that could make an impact on how you connect to people inside and outside your company.

ARTICLE 7: POWER TO THE CUSTOMER

Challenges your perceptions of what constitutes CRM success and provides real measurements for ensuring it. This section encourages conversations about the perceptions and measurements you are using to assess the health of your business relationships.

ARTICLE 8: POWER TO THE INSTRUMENT

Addresses the role of CRM tools and applications as enablers of the CRM strategy. This section encourages conversations around tool selection and use, in alignment with the relationship-building processes you have placed at the heart of your business.

ARTICLE 9: POWER TO THE VERTICAL

Offers important considerations for customizing CRM to fit the needs of your industry. This section encourages conversations about the level of effort needed to make CRM tools work within your industry and business, and the necessary investments to make it work.

ARTICLE 10: POWER TO THE ENDEAVOR

Encourages you to undertake the mandates that can

transform your company and the lives of people. It encourages conversations about how to make CRM about more than transactions and metrics and into an effort that impacts the lives of people inside and outside your immediate circles of influence.

HOW TO USE THIS BOOK

The use of the words "encourages" and "conversation" to describe each chapter is intentional. This book is intended to encourage and motivate you to see CRM as a good thing. It encourages you to engage others in conversations that lead to collaboration. Use it before you launch any CRM strategy or engage in discussions about a company-wide CRM efforts or technology implementation. Having an understanding of what CRM is, some of the misconceptions about its application, and the central themes of collaboration, relationship building, and critical interactions will give you a better foundation from which to start.

Use it when you need to re-assess your strategy. Businesses grow and change, and with change comes a need to reassess the direction of your initiatives to align with the new goals. Test your CRM strategy against the precepts of the book to determine if there is consensus and collective support before you take the next step.

Use it when things are not progressing. Remember that this book is about conversation (communication) and collaboration. Lack of shared vision, and unclear expectations, can derail any effort. Leverage the conversation and collaboration themes in this book to get everyone moving together, clarify expectations, ask questions within actionable forums that help resolve them, and discussing solutions for succeeding together.

While there are a number of compelling books about CRM available to you today, I believe this book is the first focused on encouraging standard and purposeful dialog about CRM across your company and in an open collaborative forum.

Zig Ziglar said that, "the foundation stones for a balanced success are honesty, character, integrity, faith, love and loyalty." While some of these terms are sometimes excluded from business conversations, and while some of you may find them uncomfortable to utter at work, they are nonetheless a big part of this book. I talk about being loyal and accountable to customers and about showing sincere love for the people who care about them. I talk about having faith in people and I encourage you to assess with character and integrity the reasons why you do what you do. That's because without a foundation of accountability, integrity, and trust none of what we do in sales, marketing or support would be possible.

ARTICLE 1:

INTRO TO A MANIFESTO

WE WILL NOT MAKE CRM ONLY ABOUT TECHNOLOGY, BUT ABOUT THE EFFORTS, IDEAS, PROCESSES, PRACTICES, AND TOOLS THAT HELP BUILD GENUINE RELATIONSHIPS WITH OUR CUSTOMERS AND THE PEOPLE WHO HELP THEM FEEL REWARDED FOR DOING BUSINESS WITH US.

```
man·i·fes·to noun \ˌma-nə-ˈfes-(ˌ)tō\ a
written statement declaring publicly the
intentions, motives, or views of
its issuer[1]
```

"Make the Revolution a parent of settlement, and not a nursery of future revolutions." – Edmund Burke

Tensions had been running high for two weeks before the events that brought the project to its knees. We sat together in the executive conference room – never used for this project before; only the buzzing fan of a video projector broke the silence. On one side of the table sat the project manager and the leadership team of my company, which had been hired to implement the technology. Next to them, sat the IT director and three senior members of another company who had helped build the vision of customer relationship strategy for sales and customer service. On the other side of the table sat three people I had never met before and the manager of the inbound call center. I sat in the corner, anxious, curious. I knew things had not been going as expected and this was a clear sign that something had to be addressed immediately.

One of the people I had not recognized earlier spoke up. He looked directly at the IT director and said, "I will just come out and state the obvious. We are not happy and we are not leaving this room until you do something about it." What came next I can only describe as an explosion of words and angry sentiment from both sides that would seem at times to approach resolution, before taking a turn in an even more frantic direction. For the first time in an endeavor already six months in progress, the people creating a vision of customer relationship management strategy and the people expected to implement it were meeting face-to-face to define the impact this effort would have in their business, work life, and the customer.

In the years since that meeting, I have a part of many just like it. I usually sit in a different corner: an advocate corner. An advocate for both sides struggling desperately to define the processes that will help them serve customers better. An advocate for the validity of the needs both sides have for clearer visibility across all areas of the business. What I see from that corner still makes me anxious and more eager than ever to work with people to whom customer relationship management (CRM) is more than a strategy, or a technology innovation, or a business process. The view from that corner is of business owners and managers trying to discover the best ways to run their businesses through accurate reporting and management of the pipeline that infuses it. It is of managers trying to improve on the methods that help give customers the products and services they need, while caring for the work life and work environment of people working long hours to succeed together. The landscape is of people genuinely concerned for the happiness and satisfaction of clients and the improvement of their quality of life. To them it is not just about selling, marketing, or customer care. It is about connecting the elderly with the right caregiver; it is about matching a low-income family with the correct programs; it is about helping law enforcement establish a reliable database of offenders. But in the process of designing strategies for improvement and implementing them, CRM becomes something else altogether.

It becomes a thing, a technology; it becomes a cold initiative that stops taking into account that the very components of its name are about people and relationships and managing the moments of significance and human connection that make it what it is. In its falling away from a relationship building practice, the people charged for its definition and those tasked with its execution stop working together. They become two factions holding close to their belief that one side does not understand the importance of business intelligence and process, while the other does not care for their contribution. One side struggles to learn about their best customers and the practices that lead to increased opportunities and sales that keep the company alive. The other resents being excluded from decisions that could make it more difficult for them to do their job. Both sides look across that invisible conference table with concerns that affect more than just business initiatives, sales opportunities, marketing campaigns, or customer service programs; they affect the lives of real people in a real world.

My role as a corporate relationship advocate (one who advocates that all the people that support the customer work together like the members of one body) brings me to this tragic scene often too late. Like a triage nurse, I have to decide which areas are too far-gone and which require immediate attention. It can be discouraging knowing that these mistakes disconnect the strategy from its beneficiary, the customer from the relationship, the management from the human touch. We become combatants for a cause that can never succeed; for it is counterintuitive to make a "people" strategy solely about transactions, and it is counterproductive to use technology to avoid talking to people. It only serves to perpetuate the separation of two sides that are working together towards precisely the same goal: engaging people in conversations that lead to genuine, mutually beneficial, heartfelt service.

If that were the focus, CRM would become a vehicle to connect all our corporate teams (internal and external partners and channels) with the vision of improving the central relationships of our business through meaningful interactions. CRM would become the first and most foundational step in a series of interconnected strategies that start with defining the relationship and progresses towards customer engagement, customer centricity, customer service, customer transparency, and customer experience strategies. CRM would become the table we gather around to collaborate, improve our understanding of the customer, become more appreciative of the people and components that make it happen, and generate practical   strategies that have relationships as their common end.

A CRM REVOLUTION

There is a lot we know about CRM. For many people, CRM means software and so they tend to think of it only in terms of configuration. CRM has plenty of tools and more are being developed as you read this. Because of the widespread use of CRM tools, CRM also has many consultants, experts, and gurus and many trained resources. CRM efforts have project plans, business analysis documents, and strategic narratives.

What CRM lacks is a manifesto. A manifesto that aligns the use of the tools and the goal of the professionals leading CRM efforts all over the planet. You, of course, need methodologies and planning guides, but where analysis documents help us clarify our business processes, manifestos help us declare our intentions, motives, and views. Manifestos communicate our willingness to accept new ideas and challenge the status quo. Manifestos urge us not to accept preconceptions and to promote new ideas with prescriptive notions for enacting change. Manifestos are about making a stand.

In the few hours it will take to read this book, I want you to make a commitment to a cause worth fighting. No matter the side of the table where you sit, lack of collaboration and failure to improved your business relationships should concern you. It should motivate you to change things regardless cost and the sacrifice it takes to make it right; because, if this is only about numbers, and data, and transactions in a database, and about analytics that make you feel safe, then it is not worth doing.

Now more than ever, CRM leaders need to speak frankly about the damage we have caused by misusing the term to sell software. It is time to band together to leverage what we have learned in the past ten years and use technological advancements to support customer strategies holistically, rather than the other way around. It is time to speak frankly about our need to collaborate in sharing the idea of customer relationship advocacy and placing its execution in the hands of the people that can positively affect its outcome.

For years I have been sharing the following list of "manifesto articles" with my clients. In "town hall" style meetings, project launches, and leadership calls, I encourage companies to go through the list together and set the right expectations from the start. The articles transcend industry, geography, language, company size, and technology platform. The manifesto "articles" are designed to help people across the entire company align behind a single vision of what CRM accomplishes and how it connects to other customer engagement and service initiatives that result in positive customer experiences: :

1. CRM will be about the strategies that help you build genuine relationships with customers and the people who help them feel rewarded for doing business with us (employees, partners, suppliers, etc.). Everything else, including technology, are but tools that help make that happen.

2. CRM will represent all Customer Experiences, Relationship Building, and Interaction Management

initiatives. It will be the effort under which we work together to build genuine relationships and experiences with customers.

3. CRM will not be an isolated effort. It will belong to the collective body of our company who will collaborate and commit to the goal of company-wide success.

4. CRM will become our vehicle for relationship building. We will not view people as transactions. We will acknowledge that, like in every human relationship, customer relationships follow patterns of growth and deterioration to which we must tend.

5. We will create business processes that make our interactions with people intentional. We will be mindful of the impact our interactions have on the lives of people and the life of our business.

6. We will make the customer's perception of success our measurement for CRM success. Success is when a customer feels they were able to accomplish what they needed / wanted, and that your company made it easy for them to do it; an accomplishment we measure throughout the customer experience.

7. We will not become servants to the tools that power CRM. We will choose the tools that best enable us to build relationships and measure our ability to serve customers.

8. We will improve CRM by continuously incorporating the business processes that make our industry and business

successful; constantly alert to best practices across other industries.

9. CRM discussions will be frank and transparent. We will promote an environment where we can discuss our differences and align our expectations.

10. We will make CRM an investment and consciously endeavor to improve the lives of our customers, employees, and our business.

Manifestos kindle the fire of revolution. In the case of CRM, and remembering that so many CRM initiatives meet an unsightly end, revolution is fitting. Revolution (from the Latin "revolutio", a turnaround or "revolver" to revolve) is a fundamental change in power or organizational structures. A manifesto is the tool that unites people in inciting change and sometimes it takes a revolutionary attitude to implement it. We have to at least be ready for a turnaround in our approach to CRM. One thing is certain, that you must ignite swift and immediate changes to make CRM a success for your company. This is change the CRM industry requires to shake-off the unwanted notoriety earned through years of basing CRM strategy and technology on transactions rather than the needs of people (employees and customers).

If you believe this, and are willing to embrace this book as a public declaration of CRM policy and aim, then you will join a group of brave people resolute to make CRM whole again.

Let's speak frankly about Customer Relationship Management...!

ARTICLE 2

POWER TO THE ACRONYM

WE WILL NOT FEAR THE ACRONYM, BUT USE IT AS THE BANNER UNDER WHICH WE MARCH TOGETHER TOWARDS A BETTER UNDERSTANDING OF THE PROCESSES THAT IMPROVE OUR BUSINESS RELATIONSHIPS AND EXPERIENCES.

ac·ro·nym noun \ˈa-krə-ˌnim\: a word formed from the initial letter or letters of each of the successive parts or major parts of a compound term[2]

"A lost person or article is still what it is, still valuable in itself, but in the wrong place, disconnected from its purpose and unable to be or do whatever it is intended to be or do." - David Winter, *What's in a Word*

You have probably read a number of definitions for the term "customer relationship management" or CRM:

"Customer relationship management (CRM) is a widely implemented model for managing a company's interactions with customers and prospects. It involves using technology to organize, automate, and synchronize business processes—principally sales activities, but also those for marketing, customer service, and technical support." - Dr. Robert Shaw's book "Computer Aided Marketing & Selling" (1991).

"The overall goals are to find, attract, and win new clients, service and retain those the company already has, entice former clients to return, and reduce the costs of marketing and client service." 2009 Gartner Inc. article entitled "What's 'Hot' in CRM Applications in 2009" by Ed Thompson.

"Customer relationship management describes a company-wide business strategy including customer-interface departments as well as other departments." - DestinationCRM.com

While viewed from different stages of CRM technology and practice, these definitions agree on one very important point: CRM is about managing your interactions with customers. In spite of the changes to the companies selling CRM software and consulting services, the purpose of CRM has never changed. Over the years, companies have used different methods for maintaining customer information (from paper file folders to the 360 degree-based technology we use now). But the idea that the customers are the life-blood of our businesses, that we must have a strategy for establishing the correct relationships with them, and that we must be intentional about how we manage our interactions with them has remained consistent for centuries.

However, the acronym CRM is under scrutiny. After a long debate about the use of the word "contact" for a strategy that manages customer relationships, we began a campaign that resulted in the use of "customer relationship management" as the preferred label of the industry. Then came trouble in the form of highly publicized reports about CRM high-failure rates.

Studies conducted by reputable companies like Gartner, AMR, and Forester, in collaboration with companies using the technology, published reports stating that between 2001 and 2009 as many as 50 percent of CRM implementations were viewed as failures from the customer's point of view, when asked the question "Did it meet expectations?"

As a result, CRM software vendors started to lobby for new terms to replace the term CRM for terms like "xRM". Likewise, customers began to use alternate terms to prevent internal decision-makers from nixing their CRM initiatives over rumors of difficult implementations, poor usability, and fragmented strategies supported by software solutions that presented serious privacy and data security concerns.

The idea of retiring the term CRM is alive, fueled by groups that want to replace it with the term "Customer Experience Management" (CEM or Cx for short). This mistake not only misses the definition of what CRM is, but also undermines the fact that customer experience is an important part of what CRM enables.

Customer Experience is a term that refers to the interactions a customer has with you, your employees, and your vendors over the life of the relationship. A healthy customer relationship relies on the customer evaluating each experience individually and collectively against other experiences with your brand. Relationships are the affiliations, associations, and connections we have or want to have with customers. A relationship is what we so eagerly aim to establish with the people that keep us in business. This includes companies that sell to customers only once because regardless of the times they sell to someone they still have to build a strategy for who their best customers are. Customer experiences are what customers use to determine if they want that relationship to grow or end. There are many terms used interchangeably to define a company's goal of building relationships that lead to mutual benefit. There are also terms like Customer Experience Management (CEM) that dive further into the channels customers use to building and strengthen those relationships. But neither Cx or CEM replace what CRM does. These are interconnected, supportive strategies we use to win and retain customers.

CRM AND CUSTOMER EXPERIENCE

One of the most illustrative stories about Cx I have heard lately comes from the Vice President, Customer Service & Sales Operations for one of America's largest wholesale distributor of business products. She shares a story of one of her top customer service agents; a woman who, by traditional customer service agent expectations, is not the friendliest or congenial person in the company. Jill (although that is not her name), receives some of the most positive feedback and customer service ratings in the company. Why? Because her customers are the managers of wholesale distribution warehouses. They are rough-around-the-edges just like Jill and ask only one thing when they call her: "Where the hell is my order?" They do not want Jill to ask them how they are doing or what they had for breakfast. They have their entire company asking for printer paper and office supplies and Jill expediently gets them the information and solutions they need.

How is it possible that Jill's customers "love her"? How is it that they credit her assistance for their continued loyalty? How is it that without the behavior that typically accompanies a "friendly" customer service experience Jill can keep her customers happy? The answer is that the customer experience (the very thing that keeps the customer with you and motivates them to recommend you) is based on factors that do not always have to do with loyalty. Or brand recognition or some of the other things we have attached to customer service excellence for years. Customer experience is about a customer's ability to get what they need from you and their perception of how you enable them to do that. The positive emotions that result from that enablement and accomplishment is what influence the customer to continue to do business with you and recommend you to others (be it directly or through the conversations they have about you within various social and conventional channels).

Many experts however emphasize that customer experience is not a strategy on its own. While it does require strategic planning to create a Cx program and address customer experience-specific needs, there is validity to the thought that the customer experience cannot be seen as a disconnected all-encompassing strategy for winning and keeping customers. Customer experience is a required component within a set of customer strategies that place the customer at the center of your business without sacrificing business needs. Customer experience is the simple, basic measurement we use to keep customers with us and motivated to recommend us to others. CRM is the foundation for asking the right questions about the experience, planning and connecting the interactions that compose it, and viewing the experience across everything we do with customers across the business. CRM is where Cx architecture begins and where we can most effectively gather the information needed to evaluate it.

MANY STRATEGIES, ONE FOCUS: THE CUSTOMER

There are, in fact, many other customer strategies we address independently to the detriment of unified customer strategic success. And not just disconnected from CRM, but disconnected from all the efforts you make to win, keep, or regain the customer. While one side of your company works on centralizing access to customer information, another works on the communication channels your customers use to reach you while yet another creates metrics around the customer experience. Unfortunately, these organizations often work in silos, never collaborating on their efforts to win the customer, although all along sharing that vision.

Psychologist Abraham Maslow is credited for saying "I suppose it is tempting, if the only tool you have is a hammer, to treat everything as if it were a nail." Such is the temptation for organizations to focus on what they know, and overlook what is happening elsewhere in the company. The truth is that there are many well-intended people in your company doing the right things. They are simply not working together to understand the planets in the customer strategies universe that revolves around the customer.

1. A unified approach to Customer Strategies helps you invest in the right resources, methods, and technology. But they have to support your core business strategies first. Such as your value proposition to customer segments, the channels you use to sell your products and services, the finances that fund it, and the key resources, activities, and partnerships that keep your business running. This is what allows sales, marketing, and support organizations to support both your customer and the needs of the business.

2. First, Customer Relationship Strategies help you determine the right customers for your business so you can truly invest and care for them.

3. Then, Customer Engagement Strategies help define the best ways to connect to customers through channels that facilitate clear communication. It is like building a bridge that lets customers get to you from where they are.

4. With a strong customer engagement foundation, you can make each interaction intentional and Customer-Centric. Remember, people want you to treat them as if they are your only customer.

5. You can now develop Customer Service strategies that define the level of service you can and will provide to

customers.

6. All of this delivered in a way that is transparent to the customer. All they see is a single company brand dedicated to a seamless experience for everyone.

7. From here, Customer Experience strategies monitor and ensure that customers are able to accomplish what they needed when they came to you to begin with so you can maintain positive, memorable experiences that motivate customers to buy and recommend you to others.

These are the strategies that work together to make the customer feel rewarded for doing business with you.

IT'S ABOUT EXPECTATIONS

Where, then, is the disconnect regarding the continued role of CRM as a (very much alive) customer strategy? It is in forgetting that the studies that instilled such lack of confidence in CRM did not debate the use of the acronym or its definition, and most certainly not its value. Rather, they asked frankly: did it meet expectations? It was on the responses to that question, "did it meet expectation?", the negative sentiment relied on. While a great number of CRM projects meet deadlines and are launched successfully, those responsible for rating its success do not deem it as meeting their expectation.

The misuse of terms and studies, and the rhetoric of so-called gurus about what CRM is and is not, have made CRM unrecognizable from its original self and disconnected from its purpose, unable to perform as intended. But rather than do away with the acronym or replace it with something else, we have a responsibility to address the expectation problem. We must answer that question honestly. Did CRM fail or have we been trying to meet the wrong expectations all along?. CRM has always been: A vehicle to connect all the people in your company with the vision of improving the central relationships of your business through meaningful interactions.

The acronym is just a flag under which we march to accomplish this purpose. Being hung up on the acronym will only distract you. There are, after all, more than one hundred and twenty definitions you can choose from to define what the letters stand for. Tied for number one are "customer relationship management" and "crew resource management." That does not change what CRM is.

While in my previous example the expectation was to have Jill get to the point, a customer calling you to learn about a healthcare plan or their Medicare benefits expects far more compassion and empathy. Whatever the scenario, CRM must support the customer experience and address customer expectations. You have to help people get what they need. And as a company, you have to make it easy for them to interact with you. For hospitality companies where customer experience depends on face-to-face conversations and interactions, a lot of the focus is on training people to behave correctly and understand the expectations guest have under certain circumstances (hotel check in, response time, etc.).

Same is true about training customer service agents to focus on understanding customer needs. However, in a world of increasing communication and interaction channels, customer expectation also includes their expectation to reach you via the channels most accessible to them. As a consumer, you experience this daily. You feel it when you engage a new company expecting to be able to chat with an agent on your mobile phone or tablet while waiting at the DMV and realize they have not created a channel for you to do that. Most people simply go to a competitor who can communicate with them via the channels most available to them. Otherwise, you have to communicate the value of directing them to the channels you want them to use.

As with any discipline that must factor-in people's emotional responses, customer experience depends heavily on listening. You have to listen to customers and understand what they need. You have to address the expectations they bring to the interaction. You have to build the channels customers expect to use to communicate with you. And while there is no technology silver bullet for customer experience, technology tools like CRM are a necessity in a technology savvy customer world.

IT TAKES A VILLAGE

Focusing on labels also has the adverse effect of taking the attention away from the people who contribute to the customer-centric CRM effort. CRM is not just a strategy to address the needs of the customer, but also the needs of all the people that help you serve them.

Already mentioned is the idea that the customer relationship effort is the responsibility of the entire body of people working together to serve the customer. A "corporation" from the Latin word "corpus" or "body" is a group of people united or regarded as united in one body. The idea of "customer relationship" management helps us keep the focus on the people at the heart of our effort, the customer. The idea of a body of people working together acknowledges that CRM is a strategy that aims to identify and group the whole body of people collaborating to serve the customer. The error of our current approach is not that we put the customer first. It is that we ignore the people who collectively help win and keep them loyal.

In CRM, it is the relationships among the various members of the "corpus" and their relationship to the customer (jointly) that make an impact in your ability to identify leads, manage sales processes, sell product, and deliver quality customer service. The customer experiences CRM supports are managed by everyone in the company. The shift to the mindset of the various corporate relationship entities managing the customer experience allows you to build strategies that reveal new insight into how to best serve them:

• CRM is not only about the interaction of one person with the customer. It is about the interactions of the "corpus" with the customer and each other. Often overlooked are the important conversations.

- CRM tracks between employees and partners and the value of the solutions they create together when the customer is not directly involved.

- CRM manages sales, marketing, and support business workflows as well as what may seem like disconnected interactions.

But what may seem "disconnected" at a glance, can create a clearer picture of how customers behave, engage you, and respond to the way you treat them. An "isolated" conversation with a call center agent, viewed side-by-side with other "isolated" interactions may reveal proactive ways to improve that customer's experience and make your business processes more adaptive. There is no such thing as an "isolated" conversation with the customer or about the customer. It sometimes feels like people in sales, marketing, and support create completely different highways for the customer to travel. When we tackle CRM together, we stop trying to force customers to travel our path, and we become parts of THEIR journey. Because the customer journey is no longer a linear, orchestrated journey, working together allows us to communicate how to supported the customer experience on their terms and can adequately reach out to one another at the right time.

THE V-GER EFFECT

This advice to collaborate and contribute information about customer behavior comes with a warning. While good information about the customer is the goal, some company's err in the use of CRM as a repository of ALL data without a strategy for making it useful across all of its organizations and functions. It is a lot like the central theme of the first Star Trek movie (Star Trek the Motion Picture, 1979). To provide some context for those of you who did not see the movie... The crew of the Starship Enterprise encounters a spacecraft so massive that, in its journey towards earth, leaves destruction in its path. As Kirk and the crew find themselves at the center of the craft, we learn that (spoiler alert) this is, in fact, the 20th-century Earth space probe Voyager-6.

Somewhere along its journey to collect Information, an alien race modified its original mission by mistakenly thinking this vessel was designed to learn "all that could be learned" Instead of what it was specifically designed to do. As a result, the vessel, now named "Vger", grew beyond manageable measures and became destructive in its journey to fulfill its true purpose.

Some people will say that CRM is a lot like that. The original goal off a strategy for collecting meaningful information for assessing and building customer relationships becomes a destructive effort to collect customer data beyond reasonable expectations. Curiously, some companies even change the name of their CRM systems. Some do so to help people adopt CRM by aligning it with the company culture. But a number of companies do so to turn CRM into a massive repository of data that, over time, becomes unmanageable.

The idea of using CRM to manage customer marketing, acquisition, and retention information across departments is within CRM's scope. So is the idea of buying mailing lists and leveraging the power of CRM tools to identify strong prospects and clean up data. Where CRM becomes unmanageable is when it becomes all things to all people, unkempt and outdated Rolodex of customers, vendors, and anyone else with a name and address. When you use CRM that way, you disconnect it from the business processes it is intended to manage.

Managing the "what" of CRM is the only thing that will keep it structured, purposeful, and progressive. CRM is, in many ways the ever-expanding vehicle we use to collect intelligence about the relationships we want to grow, but without a focus on the business processes it manages, and a corporate perspective of its application, it becomes unmanageable.

LOOKING ACROSS THE BUSINESS

One of the most frequent questions I hear people ask at tradeshows and business conference where I speak is "How do I connect CRM to our business goals?". In 2010 Alexander Osterwalder and Yves Pigneur, supported by 470 business practitioners wrote the book "Business Model Generation." It is a handbook for visionaries, game changers, challengers, and anyone modeling new and existing businesses. It is a fantastic guide that gives companies insight into the nature of business. It is also a great instrument for designing business processes for CRM through the development of a "business model canvas" (a tool for describing, analyzing, and designing business models).

What makes Business Model Generation so applicable

to CRM is that no CRM strategy can succeed without an honest view of how CRM business processes support the foundational building blocks of every business:

- Customer Segments

- Value Proposition

- Channels

- Customer Relationships

- Revenue Stream

- Key Resources

- Key Activities

- Key Partnerships

- Cost Structure

Throughout the book, the authors stop to ask penetrating questions about how a business creates, delivers, and captures value. By asking business stakeholders to ask questions and describe through the nine building blocks how a company intends to make money, the canvas helps them focus on the most critical aspects of their business.

Customer relationship management is identified as one of the nine blocks and defined as the strategies and methods by which "customer relationships are established and maintained with each customer segment." Note that the definition does not separate CRM as an independent part of building a business, but as relational to the other building blocks that make up our business.

It is not surprising that there is such a disconnect among business stakeholders about CRM when they see CRM as belonging only to sales, marketing, or support functions. It is also not surprising that customer relationship and customer experience efforts struggle to get C-level buy-in and sponsorship when they are unable to connect its value and support to the other parts of the business.

Here is a list of the nine building blocks used in "The Business Model Canvas" and the essential alignment you must make to CRM:

CUSTOMER SEGMENTS:

By far my most favorite quote about customers comes from Dr Michael LeBoeuf, who said "every company's greatest assets are its customers, because without customers there is no company." The most fundamental question of any business is "who is my customer?" CRM allows us to answer questions about the people for whom you create value. It also allows you to identify which ones should or should not be your customer based on the level of investment you make to win and keep them. CRM allows you to divide customers into the segments your business will support and group them based on attributes such as common needs and behaviors.

The first question your company should be asking is how your organizations should be using CRM to efficiently segment your customers to validate and support your offerings and identify the types of channels and relationships you will need to support them. If your CRM strategy does not address the question "for whom are we creating value?" you have missed the most important first step in your CRM approach and communication to your business leadership.

VALUE PROPOSITION:

With a clear understanding of "who" the customer is, we can identify the value we deliver to them. CRM strategies often account for the products and services you will include in a CRM system and use for sales and opportunity management, quote, orders, and invoices. But CRM as a strategy must also answer the questions of "which one of your customer's problems are you helping to solve?" and "what bundles of products and services are you offering to each customer segment?"

These questions are more about which customer needs you are satisfying than about what specific products and services you are importing into your CRM system. Accounting for the value a service or product offers each customer segment allows you to determine related factors like price and usability. If you cannot associate value yield with the products and services you are offering to the customer, by customer segment, you may not be meeting your customer's needs.

CHANNELS:

Just as important as identifying value proposition is the vehicle you will use to deliver that value to customers. In an evolving customer economy like ours, those "channels" are not only defined by you but also by how customers want to be reached. Channels are the important customer touch points where they experience interactions with you. Your CRM strategy must plan for expedient ways to report on whom you are reaching via those channels, which channels work best and why, and how they are integrated with customer routines.

Channels are where customers create an impression of you and how much you care about meeting their needs. If your CRM strategy does not identify the channel types and phases where meaningful interactions happen, you will be unable to create processes that work for your business and make sense to the customer where they are in their relationship with you.

CUSTOMER RELATIONSHIP:

The intentional marriage of the terms "customer" and "relationship" helps us define the purpose of establishing the relationship to begin with. As the term "family relationship" establishes boundaries for the types of interactions that are encouraged or discouraged, so does the term "customer relationship." Within the customer relationship framework, we aim to establish relationships with people we want to win or keep as customers. This immediately allows us to determine who fits within our CRM strategy.

However, customer relationship also requires us to ask "what types of relationships do each of our Customer Segments expect us to establish and maintain with them?" This expectation requires thought and planning in order to deliver correctly. If your CRM strategy is not evaluating the current ways you are establishing and maintaining your customer relationships, how these processes are integrated with the rest of your business model, and how much it costs you, you may be investing in the wrong customer relationships.

REVENUE STREAM:

A February 2012 article in the New York Times[3] investigated the now popular single-cup serve coffee brewers and found that it is well within the norm to pay more than $50 per pound of coffee to use it. To many people, pods and K-Cups, which are sold in much smaller quantities, appear to have a lower cost per cup because you are only making as much coffee as you will drink. But when you compare the cost (Nespresso Arpeggio costs $5.70 for 10 espresso capsules. Folgers Black Silk blend for a K-Cup brewed-coffee machine is $10.69 for 12 pods) you realize you'd be saving money brewing a big pot of the most expensive coffee even if you throw out what you do not drink. So why are people buying more and more of them? Because of the convenience and because, to many people, the convenience outweighs the cost.

The take away from this is that more than branding strategies facilitate a company's Revenue Stream. It can also be improved and increased by a real understanding of customer behavior. As more coffee drinkers think of their morning coffee in terms of convenience, and the more efficiently we use CRM to identify, analyze, and recognize that pattern of behavior and preference, the more we can affect Revenue Stream.

Effective CRM strategies and tools facilitate Revenue Stream strategies for companies by allowing you to understand what is important to your Customer Segments. It allows you to build pricing mechanisms you can present to customers in an effort to address what they will pay to get what they need. If you do not think that Revenue Stream strategies directly affect your relationship with customers, consider the most recent struggles banking institutions are experiencing from charging administrative and usage fees to checking account customers. The same is true for companies that charge subscription and licensing fees their customers feel are unfair or that do not provide value to them (like convenience does to the users of the single-cup coffee maker). If your CRM strategy is not deployed to support your Revenue Stream strategies, and your Revenue Stream strategy does not consider how it affects the customer relationship, the mechanisms you use to make money are disconnected.

KEY RESOURCES:

As firmly stated earlier, the worst mistake any company can make about CRM is to define it primarily in terms of the technology or tools that support it. CRM requires Key Resources to make it actionable and useful as much as your business needs them to stay operational every day. CRM needs physical, intellectual, human, and financial resources to keep it running as well.

To create a CRM strategy that supports your business (all of your business) you must identify the Key Resources that will support it, including those outside of sales, marketing, and support functions. You must also identify how CRM will support those resources and must be ready to present a business case for how each of the Key Resources of your company will benefit from CRM.

KEY ACTIVITIES:

There is within each business a defined list of the most important things a company must do to make its business model work. When a CRM strategy does not align its business processes with the Key Activities that make the business work, it is in essence working counterproductively against it. CRM has the important goal of uplifting the foundational Key Activities of your business with its own set of customer relationship activities. Some of these activities may be strictly operational, such as automatically sending a thank you letter to a new customer.

Other activities may be directly associated to how a marketing organization responds to campaigns or a sales organization responds to an inquiry, or a service organization closes a support ticket. CRM activities must always align to the Key Activities a business has established to operate successfully. You will also find that a well-orchestrated CRM strategy will provide business stakeholders with valuable information about the Key Activities customers expect and could potentially be missing from the foundational business building blocks.

KEY PARTNERSHIPS:

Partnerships and alliances are what many companies depend on to make their business model work. Companies like Wal-mart and Amazon would be unable to do business without its buyers, suppliers, and distributors. Not all businesses are matrix to include external partnerships, but we all depend on internal partnerships to stay in business. CRM best practices encourage companies to disperse silos and work together from a common foundation and strategy for building customer relationships. CRM is at the very core a partnership-focused strategy. It is easier to see the value of partnerships when they provide a clear benefit like distribution efficiency, cost reduction, or geographic strategic positioning. But internal partnerships are a bit more difficult to define. Partnerships, by design, optimize the allocation of resources and activities; internal partnerships are no exception.

If your CRM strategy does not define the role of Key Partners in reducing risk and uncertainty in the customer relationship, as well as include partner-specific tools they will need to support you, your CRM plan will be missing a key strategic component for cooperation and delivery.

COST STRUCTURE:

More CRM efforts go unfunded because proponents fail to explain how it will support a company's Cost Structure than because proponents failed to sell sponsors on the attributes of a CRM strategy. Creating and delivering value, managing customer relationships, and generating revenue for your company cost money. When companies make a decision not to invest in CRM, it isn't because they do not see the importance of their relationships and experiences with clients, but because awareness of cost keeps companies healthy. There must therefore be a strong correlation between CRM and how it supports the company's Cost Structure and business model for either driving cost or driving value. You can sell the value of CRM by aligning with the cost model of your company and providing evidence of the way CRM directly impacts cost, value, or both.

When leaders listen to presentations about customer relationships and customer experience, the impact on the core building blocks of the business is their first concern. Understanding how CRM supports the business across all of its building blocks, and learning the language and perspective of sponsors and stakeholders, will allow you to have the right conversations at the highest levels of leadership and across the entire business. It will help you show that CRM is there, at every step, orchestrating the actions that hold the steps together.

A PREMATURE OBITUARY

With all of the advances in social media and mobility and the organizational responses to these ground-shifting trends, many people question whether we should still be talking about CRM at all. Some will go as far as proclaiming the death of CRM as a customer strategy. But what makes the idea of retiring CRM difficult is that it is truly throwing the baby out with the bathwater. We cannot do away with the basic premise that to win and keep customers we have to have a customer relationship strategy. Customer relationship strategies define the types of people that will benefit from our value proposition. It helps companies determine where and in whom and in what market segments they are going to invest.

It is absolutely true that the term has become more synonymous with the technology that manages sales force automation, marketing automation, and support automation within the customer lifecycle. In an evolving economy where the customer, and not the company, defines the lifecycle, the engagement, and the channels used to build that relationship, there is an increasing gap in the way the customer engagement happens and the way CRM tools work. But the conflict is not about the need for customer relationship management strategies. The question is, do we continue to use a term so closely (and mistakenly) associated with technology and software tools. Even more challenging, I think, is the question "what is the right term to use." What is a good all-inclusive term that accurately embraces. the strategies that help us win and keep customers?

I am personally a proponent of using the term "Customer Relationship Strategies" because it points to the "customer" as the entity with whom we want to build the relationship, and it preserves the idea that a "relationship" is the ultimate goal (ideally a loyal and healthy relationship). Using the word relationship connects us back to well-grounded best practices and strategies we have used for generations to build a relationship with people. We know that relationships have patterns for growth and deterioration that we should be applying to customer relationships. Equally important, however, is that we remember that it is the customer who is in charge of the customer relationship success measure: customer experience. What we have called the "customer lifecycle" for years has not only become non-linear (it does not move nicely from lead generation, to opportunity management, to support and loyalty management anymore) but it is not (and never really was) in full control of companies.

More specifically, we do an excellent job with efforts (both strategic and technology-driven) that build functionality and accessibility, which are two of the three rating components that drive people to buy, continue to buy, and recommend you to other people. Customers ask, "Was I able to accomplish what I wanted?" and "Was it easy for me to interact with the company?" But the third component, which CRM strategies are not taking into account, is experiential; it is about customers determining how they feel about their interactions with you. Where CRM has traditionally focused on driving the customer journey, today, empowered by new culture and technology innovation, not only do people determine where that journey starts, but now the customer experience equation puts the control in the hands of the customer more than ever. They chose to purchase, continue to purchase, recommend you or switch to a competitor based on that experience or combination of experiences.

Nonetheless, the sheer number of attempts to kill and redefine CRM is a testament to its power and flexibility as an engine of business. Attempting to nail it down to "engagement" or "experience" or some other term is an attempt to hide CRM turns it into something you will be unable to successful measure. Therefore, while some companies spend millions to rename or disconnect themselves from the acronym CRM, its power as a strategy influencing collaboration in every part of the business remains its greatest strength.

ARTICLE 3

POWER TO THE COLLABORATION

WE WILL WORK COLLABORATIVELY, AS THE PART OF A COLLECTIVE BODY, WITH THE COMMON GOAL OF IDENTIFYING THE PROCESSES THAT WILL MAKE CRM SUCCESSFUL AT OUR COMPANY.

```
col·lab·o·rate intransitive verb \
kə-'la-bə-rāt\ :to work jointly with
others or together especially in an
intellectual endeavor⁴
```

"If you want to make peace with your enemy, you have to work with your enemy. Then he becomes your partner." - Nelson Mandela

An effort of such magnitude, able to unite the customer strategies across the company around the customer requires honest and heartfelt collaboration. Just as CRM enables you to see into your history with customers, so does it enable you to see across the activities and processes you conduct daily to support them together. CRM connects you to customers as much as it connects each of the people in your company to one another. It can improve your customer and internal processes with equal or greater impact if you collaborate to make it about relationships. Some of you already understand this and work in an environment where collaboration and transparency are rewarded. I congratulate you. For many companies, achieving genuine collaboration across the projects and strategies linked to CRM is a struggle. You inherited some of this struggle through the quick decisions companies sometimes have to make to acquire funding for critical functions. Sales needed a place to manage opportunities and executive leadership needed to gage the health of the pipeline. Marketing needed an efficient way to manage campaigns activities to tie ROI to sales. Support needed to modernize their case management capabilities. When the need arises organizations compete to get the funding that keeps them running, often at the expense of something else. But since then, the world of the customer has changed. The new world of the people keeping you in business requires that you work together or die in the arms of the old ways. The "new ways" require a shared vision and, in the worse cases, a truce between the warring factions that prevent its inception.

But behind the discord that sometimes exists between section managers about what CRM will accomplish for their particular departments, and the opposition from employees to change their business processes and tools are legitimate concerns that all parties must address together. Empathy for the needs of each department and the organization as a whole, coupled with the needs of the individuals implementing the practices, can lead to profitable dialog on how to make CRM successful for everyone. It is common to see CRM as the pet project of someone with power or someone who brought the concept from their previous company. Or as something managers do to create reports and dashboards that do nothing for anyone but the company's top executives. Not unlike other technical implementation initiatives, some of the friction comes from people feeling that they were left out of the process altogether. This perception is accurate much too often, a result of poor communication and lack of company-wide participation in customer advocacy efforts. But to label it as malicious or intentional is not as accurate. What is closer to the truth is that, for the most part, the people charged with making CRM initiatives successful have the same concerns as the rest of the company. Although those concerns are more about supporting the nine business building blocks we discussed earlier. These are concerns focused on keeping the business profitable and in some extreme cases, keeping doors open for business. Unless the people running the company connect the value of CRM to the business goals and support it enthusiastically, CRM cannot succeed.

COLLABORATION: THE ONLY ALTERNATIVE

Reports from Forrester Research Inc. show that companies who follow best practices for high-level sponsorship, end-user adoption, and usability, and those who consistently stay the course when it comes to developing and rolling out CRM projects across the organization, are succeeding. The Forrester study, supported by more recent studies, drew from interviews with executives at 22 large North American companies to learn about their CRM successes. All 22 saw increased revenues, lower costs, higher ROI and improved competitive strength, thanks to following CRM best practices that include:

• Strong executive sponsorship of the program

- CRM leadership collaboration with IT

- A governance structure that fosters accountability and decision-making across the entire company

- Strong executive sponsorship of the program Customer-focused defined objectives and processes in place, before applying the right technology

- Following a realistic pace for the rollout

As summarized by Bill Band, the Forrester report's project leader, staying the course together is one of the most important lessons for CRM success:

"The companies [in the study] all said they developed a long-term vision and did one country at a time, one function at a time. 'CRM in 90 days, implemented and done,' that really is a fallacy. It speaks to the over-hype in early '90s when people had visions of quick and easy return and it's just not there."

I wish that everyone could see things from my vantage point. It is a position that allows me to step back and see the hard work and even personal struggles that the entire company goes through to make CRM work. The company executives are expected to work together to assess and implement strategies and technologies appropriate to the goals, needs and business processes of the company. While department heads work hard to manage their teams, either empowered or encumbered by the same leaders, to meet objectives that are closer to the customer.

CRM can be a bridge between both corporate goals and empowering people across the company to deliver exceptional customer experiences. Sales, operations, marketing, and service leaders can come into a partnership like no other leveraging common goals that start with learning:

- How customers are being treated and want to be treated

- How customers chose to do business with you and how they want you to do business with them

- How customers learned about your products and services and...

- How customers want to stay knowledgeable (on their terms)

These are goals often unrealized because they do not include a strategy to collaborate with the employees – the people who obtain this information and feedback from the customer, or who through their experience with customers can provide this insight. Likewise, employees develop their own goals and processes in the absence of information from their leadership. Just as the CEO is working to obtain better reports about client retention, the call center agent is busy doing what he can to keep the customer happy. In the absence of an active process or tool to do that, people create their own.

While the Chief Operations Officer is busy trying to reduce the time customers wait on the phone, the customer service specialist is listening empathetically to the mom who needs as much time as necessary to find a same-day appointment for her sick child. Without collaboration the people investing in CRM and the people implementing it work against each other without intending to. Without collaboration the customer ultimately walks away feeling that you are not working together to help them with their needs and making it easy for them to do business with you.

To create and deploy the correct strategy and technology that helps companies win and keep customers, you have to collaborate. The people who make the decisions, the people who use the technology, the people who interact with customers, the people who provide them service, the people who help customers feel rewarded for doing business with you, the people who collaborate daily with one another to meet customer needs... they ALL have to work together to enjoy success together.

THE CRM EYE EXAM

I have never enjoyed the yearly trip to the eye doctor to get my eyes checked. It is not the actual exam that irritates me but the number of people involved. One person checks my records and signs me in; another performs the pre-exam before the optometrist takes me into the big chair. There my eye doctor will get uncomfortably close to my face, shine a light that must have been designed for use with lighthouses in the Eastern seaboard, and switch suspiciously similar lenses in front of me to determine if I can see better with one or two.... one, or two. Then, as

I stumble blindly back into the reception area with giant dilated pupils, yet another person begins the process of helping me select contact lenses and/ or frames.

Last year I noticed something that had escaped me in previous years. When Denise, the eye care technician, takes me to the "great wall of frames" to choose my frames, she always asks me to take off my glasses. What follows is the ridiculous exercise of making decisions about what I look like in the new frames without being able to actually see. Seems a little crazy, but we all do it. We make decisions about our eyewear while wearing frames providing no vision at all. It is no surprise that, when the frames come back with the correct lenses, our opinion of them is so different. Lately, I have been taking my wife with me for an unbiased opinion. Even Denise jumps in and shares her thoughts, and ultimately the decision I make is far more educated and unbiased. This collaboration has saved me from embarrassing myself many times. I know that I am the one who needs to make the decision about how these new glasses will fit my lifestyle and allow me to interact with my world, and the people I bring into it, but it is a lot easier to recruit help when my vision is unclear.

I have come to appreciate one very important thing about the yearly visit to the eye doctor, that the business of vision is a collaborative effort that requires multiple individuals, all helping me see better, when my vision is weak and obstructed. It is at the time when I can see the least that I count on every person involved in this process to help me correct my vision, maintain healthy vision, and select the right tools for keeping my vision clear.

I shared this analogy with a friend recently and she told me that a major retailer of eyewear in the United States has a system that photographs you wearing the frames of your choosing, and then allows you to look at pictures of yourself wearing them. Another retailer allows you to upload pictures and do the same thing online before you even get to the store. There is even a "Style Survey" that lets you choose glasses that fit your personality: "What is your idea of a dream vacation?" "Which shoes best reflect your style?" "What's your idea of a perfect night out?" A very helpful system, but only a part of a larger process because frames do not improve your eyesight but make it easier for you to wear your glasses. They are only a part of the equation that allows you to apply individuality and style to a vital need, the need to see properly. Incidentally this is a fitting comparison to the way some companies focus on the selection of CRM technology and stylish marketing websites without focus on what they are intended to do for customers.

The correct approach to correcting and improving your vision is to work together to examine the myopic and nearsighted vision that affects your business as a team with unique perspectives and roles and answers. And yes that includes the people that help you look good in those jazzy spectacles.

Some of you reading this are preparing to try on some new eyeglasses. Some of you are regretting the set you already chose. Some of you are realizing you never even bothered to get your vision checked. As with my own visit to the eye doctor, it always helps to have the right people involved who understand what to check. That help must come from people within your company who can impartially provide vision corrections and simultaneously consider the importance of the voice of the customer and how they see you.

Only through that collaboration can you make the right decisions about where CRM fits your company vision and how to implement it.

ADAPTIVE CHALLENGES AND WICKED PROBLEMS

Only through collaboration can we resolve problems that fall under what author Craig Weber defines as "adaptive challenges." In his book "Conversational Capacity"[5] Craig writes about both "routine" problems and "adaptive" problems saying:

"Routine problems may be painful, expensive, and frustrating, but we have the advantage of knowing what to do about them and how to work through them. We have, in other words, a routine for dealing with them. Contrast a routine problem with an adaptive challenge. An adaptive challenge is a problem for which we have no ready solution, no expert we can call upon to guide us through, no clear way forward. We have, in other words, no routine. We know we're facing an adaptive challenge when we find ourselves in unfamiliar territory with no mental map of our predicament. Lost in uncharted terrain, we must pull together with the people around us to make sense of the hard realities we're facing and successfully adapt to the new environment."

In "Dilemmas in a General Theory of Planning"[6], urban planners Horst Rittel and Melvin Webber talk about problems that are "ill-defined" by calling them "wicked problems." Wicked problems are those that do not have a definable and separable solution. Wicked problems are, well, never solved. At best, they are only re-solved over and again. Rittel and Webber were specifically addressing the challenges involved in making decisions within immensely complex social circumstances (such as the decision-making required to achieve sound public policy or urban design). But they also used the term to expand on the problems that face interdisciplinary collaboration. Collaboration is a wicked problem because, as Rittel and Webber define it, collaboration has no definitive preparation; they have no common rules, no ultimate test for the solution, and each collaboration yields its own specific and fitted results. With collaboration, we learn with each trial and error and each attempt is significant in contributing to the solutions we forge together. Each collaboration is unique and without limits for the number of benefits it can yield.

But don't you already know all this? Has your company not spent thousands of dollars over the years to motive everyone to join forces, team up, and think of the intellectual investment others make to the collective? Collaboration is not always prevented by lack of knowledge of what it takes to do it, but by holding firm to the mistaken belief that we are the only ones who "get it". The dose of realism we must inject into our customer efforts is that too many people are making decisions without seeing the whole elephant as illustrated in one of my favorite poems, "The Blind Men and the Elephant" by John Godfrey Saxe (1816-1887):

It was six men of Indostan
To learning much inclined,
Who went to see the Elephant
(Though all of them were blind),
That each by observation
Might satisfy his mind.

The First approached the Elephant,
And happening to fall
Against his broad and sturdy side,
At once began to bawl:
"God bless me! but the Elephant
Is very like a WALL!"

The Second, feeling of the tusk,
Cried, "Ho, what have we here,
So very round and smooth and sharp?
To me 'tis mighty clear
This wonder of an Elephant
Is very like a SPEAR!"

The Third approached the animal,
And happening to take
The squirming trunk within his hands,

Thus boldly up and spake:
"I see," quoth he, "the Elephant
Is very like a SNAKE!"

The Fourth reached out an eager hand,
And felt about the knee
"What most this wondrous beast is like
Is mighty plain," quoth he:
"'Tis clear enough the Elephant
Is very like a TREE!"

The Fifth, who chanced to touch the ear,
Said: "E'en the blindest man
Can tell what this resembles most;
Deny the fact who can,
This marvel of an Elephant
Is very like a FAN!"

The Sixth no sooner had begun
About the beast to grope,
Than seizing on the swinging tail
That fell within his scope,
"I see," quoth he, "the Elephant
Is very like a ROPE!"

And so these men of Indostan
Disputed loud and long,
Each in his own opinion
Exceeding stiff and strong,
Though each was partly in the right,
And all were in the wrong!

MORAL.
So oft in theologic wars,
The disputants, I ween,

Rail on in utter ignorance
Of what each other mean,
And prate about an Elephant
Not one of them has seen!

The most tragic flaw in your customer-centered strategies may be that you do not have a clear picture of what your customer actually looks like. You formulate your opinions based on a partial view and limited knowledge of customers without a comprehensive understanding that can only come from your collective knowledge of the customer. It raises questions about how people who have an incomplete picture of the customer can make customer relationship, engagement, or experience management decisions without meaningful collaborations across the company. We speak so boldly about an elephant we have never seen entirely.

CRM success requires that you work together to identify the routine and solve the adaptive. You have to work together to understand the problems that are most usual in your interactions with customers, and (through the support of the right analytics) learn what causes them, when, and how people throughout your company are resolving them. Likewise, you have to collaborate to respond to adaptive challenges. These are more difficult to address because by definition adaptive challenges are those for which we do not have a process. An unmanaged adaptive challenge can kill your business and requires that everyone put aside their differences and even admit to creating the problem. Collaborating on the strategy and practice of CRM is indeed a "wicked problem." It surfaces challenges and discussions with people from multiple skill sets, competencies, agendas, and goals that sometimes seem insurmountable and results in wounded egos and challenging conversations.

One of the best ways to engage collaboratively around the customer challenges CRM solves is through what Michael P. Farrell refers to as "collaborative circles" in his book "Collaborative Circles: Friendship Dynamics and Creative Work"[7]:

"A collaborative circle is a set of peers in the same discipline who, through open exchange of support, ideas, and criticism develop into an interdependent group with a common vision that guides their creative work"

"Creative work is rarely done by a lone genius. Artists, writers, scientists and other professionals often do their most creative work when collaborating within a circle of like-minded friends. Experimenting together and challenging one another, they develop the courage to rebel against the established traditions in their field. Working alone or in pairs, then meeting as a group to discuss their emerging ideas, they forge a new, shared vision that guides their work. When circles work well, the unusual interactions that occur in them draw out creativity in each of the members."

However, rather than restricting participation to like-minds and people with complementing competencies, the collaboration circle we are talking about is a "sharing circle". One in which you share what you know about the customer to help others paint a complete picture. The types of conversations you are having today to make CRM tools available to sales, marketing, and support are part of one circle. In that circle, you talk about the customer as an individual about whom you are collecting information. You talk about the customer in its most relational form so that you can connect information about them from the right sources, in a manner that keeps that information secured and free of duplicates. Those are important conversations in your circle, if your role is to implement a CRM tool. But unless you understand how each person in your company interacts with the customer, how they take care of customer needs, what challenges they experience in creating a positive customer experience, then your view of the customer is incomplete. You have to collaborate with the people that can help complete that picture.

CRM collaboration cannot amount to a bunch of meaningless tasks in a CRM implementation project plan. Here is where we often realize that we have to talk to people throughout the company to design the business processes that will drive CRM workflow. Here is also where many of the contributors to that analysis learn for the first time that a CRM project is even in progress. CRM collaboration cannot take place in isolation in corporate boardrooms where executives decide the reports they need to run the business without feedback from the people physically interacting with the customer. It cannot happen without an understanding of customer needs from the customer himself.

CRM collaboration cannot fix internal business process challenges if it leaves out the people for whom CRM was created (and I am talking about the customer, not sales). It cannot be something you do strictly for the sake of improving operational efficiencies unless it improves the customer experience and is connected to all the people creating that experience. As Jeremy Bentham put it, "It is the greatest good to the greatest number of people which is the measure of right and wrong." Or as Spock would say, "The needs of the many outweigh the needs of the few."

What, then, are the customer-centric things you should be gathering to talk about and collaborate about?

RETIRING THE SILOS

Wikipedia reports that at its peak in 1967, the stockpile of nuclear warheads owned by the Unites States came to an alarming 31,265 warheads. It is estimated that, since 1945, the United States produced more than 70,000 nuclear warheads, which is more than all other nuclear weapon states combined. The Soviet Union/Russia has built approximately 55,000 nuclear warheads since 1949, France built 1110 warheads since 1960, the United Kingdom built 835 warheads since 1952, China built about 600 warheads since 1964, and other nuclear powers built less than 500 warheads altogether since they developed their first nuclear weapons.[8] There are thousands of nuclear silos all over the world (active and inactive), yet, the Oxford English Dictionary uses the following examples first to help explain what a "silo" is:

"It's vital that team members step out of their silos and start working together [AS MODIFIER]: we have made significant strides in breaking down that silo mentality."

"Most companies have expensive IT systems they have developed over the years, but they are siloed why are so many companies still siloing their SEO and social media marketing?"

"Managers have been told to break down the walls between siloed applications."

That's because the "silo" mentality is a common and devastating problem we face every day. It is created when people refuse (intentionally or unintentionally) to share information with others. It is the mentality that most often reduces operational efficiency, collaboration, and even morale.

CUSTOMER RELATIONSHIP SILOS:

Contributing to a centralized view of customers worries salespeople because they fear someone else will sell to their prospects or intrude on a relationship they have worked so hard to establish. When salespeople keep personal and sales activity information about customers to themselves, however, it creates blind spots in what should be a 360-degree view of customers. The concern over sharing contact information is not a strategy or technology problem. It is a trust problem and requires attention. If you cannot trust the people you work with to exchange information openly and collaboratively you will never be able to enjoy the benefits a unified customer strategy offers.

From a strictly practical perspective, it benefits everyone to know what is happening with a customer regardless of where they are in the sales cycle; especially if they are an existing customer already receiving marketing information or being serviced by the customer service organization. The stories you hear about sales professional calling on customers, only to find out the customer is angry at your company, are true. Of greater concern than sharing information with your peers, however, is that your customers are engaging your company via many channels and talking about it (maybe even about you) via social media. Working with all the organizations that own customer interactions and channels, the people engaging customers via social conversations, and those gathering important information about the customer (their buying preferences, expectations, and experiences with your company) is more important than ever.

CRM may only be your opportunity and pipeline management system today. Today it may only be your strategy for qualifying, pursuing leads, and closing sales. But with the right collaborations, CRM can become about truly knowing your customers. The right collaboration strategy can be the best resource for maintaining an accurate record of customer data and their interactions with your company, regardless of who they interact with at your company or where they go to learn or talk about you.

CUSTOMER ENGAGEMENT SILOS:

Elsewhere in your company, another group of people is defining how customers will engage you and via what channels. Customer Engagement strategies evaluate the most cost effective communication channels for customers to reach you and how. A strong Customer Engagement strategy also continually evaluates what channels your customers want to use to reach you. Where CRM and CEM often disconnect is in the implementation of supporting tools. CEM tools are most often implemented by call center organizations in support of customer service and support functions. It is common for sales and marketing organizations to use different tools from those used by customer service due to the complexity and investment required to implement CEM tools. While CRM tools are commonly just software, CEM tools that support the call center require interactive voice response, external customer portals, knowledge management, chat, and messaging resources.

CUSTOMER-CENTRICITY SILOS:

Over the past few years, the term "customer-centricity" has gained a lot of popularity. It is even used to describe CRM and even replace the term. In many companies, customer-centricity as a marketing-owned activity for customer segmentation and identification. However, customer-centricity is not a replacement term for CRM. And it is not just marketing's responsibility.

Author and CRM expert Don Peppers explains it this way in a recent post on his LinkedIn blog:

"What does it mean to be "customer-centric" as a business? Assuming that you start with a quality product and service, being customer-centric means understanding the customer's point of view and respecting the customer's interest. You fix problems, handle complaints, and remember individual customer preferences." "But customer-centric competition starts with an individual customer and tries to meet as many of that customer's needs as possible – across all the company's divisions and business units, and through time (i.e., meeting a customer's needs week after week, month after month)."

Customer-centricity is not a strategy disjointed from CRM. It is the component within the CRM strategy that addresses the individual needs and preferences of customers. It is the personalization of the customer experience; what you do that makes them feel that you are thinking about them and their needs specifically.

CUSTOMER SERVICE SILOS:

You cannot isolate the ideas of "relationship" and "service", however, many CRM strategies are implemented without serious consideration for what "customer service" really is. For many CRM practitioners, customer service is a modular component in a CRM application. It is something you don't implement if the Customer Service manager of your company is uninterested or if you only have enough budget. Although I have seen it happen the other way around: A company purchases a CRM system to address case management needs and leaves out the sales and marketing stakeholders.

In either case, the idea that "customer service" is an essential part of what CRM does is often overlooked. Not because people don't know what customer service is, but because they view customer service as a function and not a customer strategy that gives all the other customer strategies a charter for how to treat the customer. Customer service strategies are not just for call centers. They are for all of us. It is the set of rules we put in place that say "this is how we will treat the customer and this is what we will do when we don't". The definition of "customer services" has gradually become disconnected from the definition of "service" and the idea that the "customer" is the recipient of that service. Instead, "customer service" has become synonymous with the practices call centers use to manage their interactions with customers and the metrics that make it cost-effective to interact with them. We have created call center metrics that determine how long an agent should be on the phone and have created tools for moving the customer to more self-help activities. As a result, we detached "service" from "customer service" and today we struggle to maintain these call center success measurements while trying to deliver good customer experiences. It has become difficult for one side of your company to use call center metrics to gauge success while another measures if based on customer experience measures. One side pushes call center agents to make their interactions with customers as brief as possible while the other tells them to give the customer what they need, no matter how long it takes.

Service is contribution to the welfare of others. One of my favorite people, and the Customer Experience Officer for one of the world's leading footwear brands, has a quote on her signature block from Rabindranath Tagore:

"I slept and dreamt that life was joy. I awoke and saw that life was service. I acted and behold, service was joy."

Customer service is the strategy that brings joy with structure to all your customer strategies. It makes everyone follow the same rules for caring about your customers and tells you what you should do for them when they are not happy. It enables everyone in your company to give customers memorable experiences and it empowers them to do what they can to meet their expectations.

CUSTOMER EXPERIENCE SILOS:

The most recent culprit in our "silos" list is the concept of "customer experience". Evaluating the customer experience is, by far, one of the most effective ways for your company to understand what your customers need from you. It is an indispensable part of winning and keeping customers. For companies that have experienced unsuccessful CRM implementations, or for companies that fear CRM failure, it is easy to see customer experience as the ultimate answer. Companies that shift their attention exclusively to customer experience risk isolating the strategies that support it and feed it with necessary information and processes. I am amongst the strongest supporters of adopting customer experience measurements to assess the health of customer relationships. I am also amongst the most avid to emphasize that customer experience is a measurement we use. It is not a strategy we build independently from the customer relationship, engagement, and service strategies that jointly give you a realistic view of customers.

The right feedback by the right people can more efficiently define what you need, and ideally, helps you deliver the strategies and tools you need to serve others with greater passion and ability (both inside and outside your company).

When people work together to implement CRM, it allows it to become the foundation of a new imperative described by Harley Manning and Kerry Bodine in the book "Outside In"[9]:

"...creating and nurturing a system of interdependent, self-reinforcing practices that align employee, partners, processes, policies, and technology around customers."

To finish the CRM race, we have to run together, arm in arm. We have to set aside our own agendas and collaborate on common goals that take into account the needs of all CRM stakeholders and, most importantly, the customer.

ARTICLE 4

POWER TO THE RESOLUTION

WE WILL BE TRANSPARENT WHEN RESOLVING PROBLEMS AND WILL PROMOTE AN ENVIRONMENT WHERE WE CAN DISCUSS OUR DIFFERENCES AND ALIGN OUR EXPECTATIONS.

```
res·o·lu·tion noun \ˌre-zə-ˈlü-shən\:
the act or process of dealing with
something successfully: to progress from
dissonance to consonance¹⁰
```

"It is easy to dodge our responsibilities, but we cannot dodge the consequences of dodging our responsibilities." - Sir Josiah Stamp

The challenges companies experience undertaking CRM are not solved just by deciding to work together. They require resolve and determination, and more importantly, execution. CRM is worth doing and "whatever is worth doing at all is worth doing well" (Philip Stanhope, 4th Earl of Chesterfield). Implementing the right customer relationship strategies and tools require the type of determination that leads to open and honest dialog. The process requires the people making company-wide decisions about the business and the people enforcing and implementing those decisions to resolve their differences and answer questions that affect them both. To run a successful business, the people responsible for its operations have to make tough choices and make certain everyone adheres to the practices that keep your company doors open (and in compliance and out of legal hot water). The people selling, marketing, and supporting the business have a responsibility to follow those guidelines while maintaining a focus on creating positive customer experiences. The correct dialog allows you to address the problems that are interfering with how you run your business as well as how you take care of customers.

You already know that communication is the foundation of a strong business. However, we are talking about more than just sharing information and distributing it across the company. We are talking about having open dialog that facilitates asking the right questions of the right people; allowing everyone in your business to offer their feedback without fear of judgment or retribution. CRM efforts that do not start with frank conversations lead to almost immediate performance problems and mistrust. Something as simple as overlooking introductory dialog about your goals for the CRM effort can result in suspicion, animosity, and even resentments. Especially from people who have done this well at other companies and who feel you are are not accounting for their valuable feedback. The disconnect between what we call "communication" and true, genuine, open dialog, accounts for the failure of many CRM implementations. It is ironic that, as it relates to CRM technology implementation specifically, we spend so much time deploying the technology and so little time talking to the people who will use it. We then complain that the CRM project failed in lack of user acceptance and try desperately to correct the problem by initiating dialog with people who, by this point, feel they have been ignored.

I intentionally use the word "resolution" because this must be the goal of our customer relationship conversations: to engage in dialog that helps us deal with problems successfully; to progress from dissonance (lack of harmony) to consonance (agreement or compatibility between opinions or actions).

One of my most favorite reads is the book "Why Employees Don't Do What They're Supposed To Do and What To Do About It," by Ferdinand F. Fournies. Human resource professionals quote it often because of its usefulness to managers in determining why people do not perform as expected. The book lists the following reasons why people do not do what they are supposed to do at work:

1. They don't know why they should do it

2. They don't know how to do it

3. They don't know what they are supposed to do

4. They think your way will not work

5. They think their way is better

6. They think something else is more important

7. There is no positive consequence to them for doing it

8. They think they are doing it

9. They are rewarded for not doing it

10. They are punished for doing what they are supposed to do

11. They anticipate a negative consequence for doing it

12. There is no negative consequence to them for poor performance

13. Obstacles beyond their control

14. Their personal limits prevent them from performing

15. Personal problems

16. No one could do it

Excluding insurmountable obstacles and personal limitations common to us humans, Fournies' list describes fittingly many of the reasons people do not support CRM initiatives. Sometimes people do not see pass their own priorities, needs, or inter-departmental agendas, regardless of whether they are doing so because they want to isolate themselves or because they don't know any better. Thinking that everyone will support CRM or will simply get behind the effort because a senior executive mandates it is a dangerous assumption. People respond differently based on their knowledge of the effort and their ability to respond (based on what they think they should do or are already doing). You have to work together to take inventory of what people need in order to respond adequately to what you need them to do. What is certain is that people are going to ask questions, and the first step towards resolution is to initiate and encourage honest dialog.

Every customer relationship initiative is different and may

require more extensive investigation of the apprehensions people have about it. If you present yourself as a trustworthy advocate for both employees and customers, people will be more inclined to tell you their concerns and will bring you more frequently into the conversations they are probably already having. If you do not have visibility into what people are thinking or saying (through direct communication or via Voice the Employee survey data), you have an advantage you should leverage to answer questions in response. If you do not, here is a list of questions indispensable to CRM success which you must take a proactive approach to answer:

WHY ARE YOU DOING THIS?

People want to know the answer to a very important question, "Why?" Why the expense, why the change in a new direction that could disrupt day-to-day work life? Why now? The "why" questions is fair and reasonable from the people who will be called upon to carry the flag and make sacrifices to make CRM a success. It is also a question that helps you validate the reason you are doing this to begin with and one that you have to answer well. Addressing why you are implementing a customer relationship strategy and / or technology solution is the first part of this exercise. The second part is to listen to what happens next. It may be that people welcome your explanations with open arms. In companies that did not do their due diligence to understand what solutions were already in place, this could result in some unpleasant surprises instead. It could result in learning that there are efforts in place that will not allow you to proceed as planned. It could also be there is a history you do not know; the story of why CRM failed in the past and how people with a need to access customer information created their "own way." You may hear about the creative and innovative ways people fixed the problem, and you may get an opportunity to build that collaboration we have been talking so much about by identifying champions and subject matter experts.

For many of you reading this book, CRM is not a new thing. Not by far. You have been at multiple companies and used several different CRM solutions that have the words dynamics and act and force, or the name of mythical horses in them. You have seen them succeed and fail and have, by now, created personal preferences for the ones you like using best. With that experience, you have also gained insight into the many (sometimes ridiculous reasons) why companies choose to implement CRM. Some of you are asking the "why" question about your current company. Why did they do this? What was the long-term goal and what is the plan to leverage such a vital initiative for gaining company-wide intelligence about customer interactions? The answers to "why CRM?" cannot be only about centralizing contact records or having a place to manage your sales activity and pipeline. Not because CRM does not do that well, but because people know what CRM can do and how it can help you target the right customers with the right value proposition using very powerful tools.

Vital to the explanation you give people is the "why" CRM will support the other strategies in the customer strategy universe (engagement, centrality, service, transparency, and experience) and the customer experience ecosystem itself. People need to know that CRM strategy takes into account the things they are doing to win and keep customers, and to align it to the strategies they support is extremely important. So is the need to show people how CRM influences the customer experience and where.

WHY SHOULD WE BE A PART OF IT?

Gaining people's attention does not always mean winning their enthusiasm. Besides knowing why you are doing something, they also want to know why they should support it. Remember that CRM projects (while, in my opinion, misjudged) already have a bad reputation for low user adoption. CRM applications have been around long enough for even people who have never used them to know they have been the target of criticism. Why, then, should people jump for joy to support an effort few have implemented successfully?... Allegedly. Helping people understand why they should support customer relationship efforts is not difficult. People know that the customer is the reason you are in business and why you come to work every day. If you don't believe that, or have difficulty getting your team to believe it, read the "Power to the Customer" chapter of this book and then come back. The goal is to help people understand that CRM is a foundational part of how your company will identify the customers you can best serve, and part of how you create memorable experiences that bring them back and motivate them to recommend you to others.

The endeavor you are asking people to support is not a software implementation effort, a technology project, or business process automation effort. Even if that is the next step in the CRM strategy, you cannot make it about software tools. You are asking them to be part of a better and more intimate way to know the customer. You are building a road that accelerates how your customers engage you, how sales identifies what customers want from you, and how well you are meeting the commitments you made to them as a transparent brand. If people see CRM only as software, they will add it to the list of other things your company is implementing, and part of a longer list of things that disrupt their ability to care for customers. Participation and (better yet) collaboration requires that you align your goals and roadmap for implementing CRM with what people are already doing. You will be watch many of the tasks you thought you had to initiate yourself already live and in progress by your new advocates.

ARE YOU GOING TO TEACH ME
HOW TO DO THIS SUCCESSFULLY?

I started my CRM career many years ago as a software trainer. The software company I worked for had a fabulous catalog of certification programs we offered to users, developers, and system administrator. CRM software companies have improved software application training to make it contextual to the experience of using the software itself. Learning the tools that help you win customers is an essential part of CRM, and you have plenty of great training resources, training companies, and trainers to leverage in your CRM software education journey.

We are, however, talking about more than software training here. We are talking about skill beyond the tools and knowledge preliminary to anything you teach and learn about CRM implementation. People need to know that you have a plan for educating them in the fundamentals of CRM practice and that you will give them the skills they need to make it applicable to their areas of focus. People need to know that you plan to educate them in what customer relationship strategy is, how it helps your business, and how you will leverage it (with their help) to mobilize the processes that help them help customers. People ultimately want to know you have a plan for addressing knowledge deficiencies without putting their current efforts in jeopardy.

WHAT IS OUR ROLE?

People do not want to receive marching orders disconnected from their understanding of the larger CRM initiative. That is often the case when project managers treat people as a "task assignment" in a project plan. People want to know the role they will have in molding the strategy as stakeholders before you tell them what you expect them to contribute, to whom, when and where. Defining the role of individuals and teams in relationship to the "big picture" is extremely critical to collaboration. Helping people understand their role (or better yet, their contribution) creates a connection between what some may see as an isolated effort and the tasks they perform daily; the things of greatest and most immediate value to them.

It is no accident that this book addresses the problem of business silos and challenges of building collaboration first. Ambiguity about how you may be using technology and new processes to potentially replace current jobs is a dangerous thing for people to ponder. No one wants to be left wondering if their jobs are at risk or if you plan to replace processes they need to do their job (at least not without their involvement). No player ever goes into an NBA game wondering what position he or she will play and how their contribution will help win the game. Successful CRM strategies account for every player at every stage of the game and plan adequately for their involvement.

WHY IS "THIS" A PRIORITY?

To many people CRM is sometimes a pipe dream that interferes with their job. As a result, they face conflicting priorities about what is more important: their contribution to the CRM effort or doing their job. To the salesperson that has to meet his quota, the customer service representative that has to meet service level agreements, and the call center manager who has pressing utilization and call center metrics to support, CRM is but "another" unreasonable change coming down to them from the people upstairs.

WHY IS "THIS" INITIATIVE GOING TO WORK?

Remember that you may not be the only person within your company advocating the value of their initiative. People may be in the middle of other types of business and technology transitions (personnel changes, policy implementations, system and hardware upgrades, etc.). As a result, they face conflicting priorities about what is more important: their contribution to the CRM effort, another IT project, or doing their job. For many of the reasons we already discussed, but ultimately because CRM can serve as a vehicle to connect all your efforts to win and retain customers through positive customer experiences, you have to effectively communicate CRM value. CRM is not a rest stop in the customer experience journey. It is part of the core infrastructure of a company's customer acquisition and retention strategy.

In the last five years alone companies have introduced more new strategy approaches for CRM, change management, self-service, quality management, and enterprise planning than we have seen in the previous ten years combined. The same is true about the introduction of hardware and software technology innovation more advanced that anything we have seen in the past twenty years. It makes sense that, at this pace, you may have to fight for attention (even more so if some things did not launch with the anticipated success). Do not be surprised that some people approach CRM as another idea in a long line of failed efforts and be prepared to state your case.

SUSPEND YOUR UNBELIEF

If you are tasked with contributing to the CRM effort in any way, you share equal accountability in this matter. While your executives are responsible for engaging you in meaningful dialog that helps answer your questions and allow you to contribute your experiences, you are responsible for your part. We all have to stop acting like combatants and start acting like partners willing to share information and bring issues to final resolution. It is your support and contribution to your company's CRM effort that will make it a success. For those of you in the middle of CRM crisis, you have a choice to either invigorate a failing effort or speed its demise.

While it is true that the perception of CRM success rates is not very high, it is also true that thousands of companies worldwide experience a return on their CRM investment and achieve their goal of improving the lives of the people and the customers they serve. Every company has unique needs. They are led by people with diverse backgrounds and values, and composed of uniquely qualified groups of people. No one company is the same as the next. This may be the reason why it is so difficult to pin down CRM success and failure statistics – because no one CRM effort is the same. So suspend your disbelief until you understand what your company is doing and the goals it has set.

Because CRM has been around for a while, there is a large enough test sample population from which to draw case studies. If you ask questions, you will get answers. Seek out the forums that talk about CRM implementations (good and bad). Visit your industry water coolers and engage personally with the people who have gone through what you are going through.

TAKE OWNERSHIP

Approaching this effort with a positive and enthusiastic attitude does not mean that you agree with everything you hear. It means that you are willing to provide honest feedback and not purposely sabotage the efforts of the people trying to help it succeed. CRM is a living thing that can be deployed gradually to address the greatest needs of the company. In some cases, it may be best to deploy a centralized, unified strategy across the entire company simultaneously. In either case, there will be some sacrifices needed from all the stakeholders. Be willing to listen to all proposed approaches and have an open mind about the impact it may have on you personally.

INCREASE THE DIALOG

This book is a tool to promote and increase the dialog that must take place between the people leading the CRM process and the people helping to make it successful. Sometimes a company approaches CRM with the best of intentions but still hurts the people it is supposed to help. Through the types of questions we have discussed you can clarify and correct hindrances to communication and achieve mutually beneficial results. Sometimes the people in charge are unable or unwilling to initiate the dialog. In such cases, I encourage you to initiate. Ask others about what they have heard. Engage in conversations about what you have learned about CRM and how it can help your company. Then make every effort to talk to your leadership. Offer your support and be open to go through the questions we listed earlier.

If your company is talking about CRM at any level, and they have not initiated a conversation with you, take time to initiate the dialog yourself. Especially if your company is in the process of selecting a CRM technology partner, be aggressive in initiating a conversation about CRM because, let's face it, the burden will fall on you eventually. You have the opportunity to have a positive influence now that not only will make your life easier but the lives of everyone with whom you interact to support customers.

ARTICLE 5

POWER TO THE RELATIONSHIPS

WE WILL NOT VIEW PEOPLE AS TRANSACTIONS. WE WILL ACKNOWLEDGE THAT, LIKE IN EVERY HUMAN RELATIONSHIP, CUSTOMER RELATIONSHIPS FOLLOW PATTERNS OF GROWTH AND DETERIORATION TO WHICH WE MUST TEND.

re·la·tion·ship noun \-shən-ˌship\: the
state of being connected by reason of an
established or discoverable quality[11]

"The quality of your life is the quality of your relationships." - Anthony Robbins

Withdrawing our focus from acronyms and gimmicks, and resolving to collaborate on the CRM effort through open and sincere dialog unites us in building relationships that last. Building relationships is not only at the center of CRM; it is its foundation and purpose. As I collaborate with customers to implement the processes and technology that power their customer strategies, I am constantly reminded of the people they serve. I have to be careful not to allow meetings and project deadlines distract me from the real gaol. It is easy, in my eagerness to get to the end-result, to forget the people for whom we are working so hard. When the going gets tough, it is easy to focus on installing software, putting people through training, creating business workflows, and marking tasks as "completed." I have to go back to thinking about the customer and the people that come to work every day to be of fervid service to them.

When the focus is on people, those transactional minutes can turn into moments of exuberance and even bliss. Even more so when a product or service the company provides has a profound impact on the lives of people (even humanity as a whole). Most of you have seen CRM improve processes that help a company cut operational costs and gain market share. But have you seen it change lives? Sometimes (not often enough) CRM is about helping people meet the most fundamental needs for healthcare and human services. It is true that sometimes the customer you serve is a lawyer in New York trying to increase their portfolio of clients. But for many of you the customer you serve is a child whose life will be enriched by the improvement of childcare services in their state. It is a single mother who will be able to spend a little extra quality time with her children on her way to her third job because someone was mindful of her needs. Or the terminally ill patient who will be able to enjoy improved quality of life in his last days, a hospice caregiver committed to keeping him comfortable, or a spouse whose life will be a little easier when making final arrangements.

The common theme in what CRM does for every organization is that it helps your company focus on people. For the companies changing the world and the companies making customers happy one at a time, CRM is about building and nurturing relationships through memorable experiences. For companies swallowed up in CRM practices that bind it to technical interfaces and data transactions this is a difficult transition to make. To them, "relationship" has to do only with the way relational databases maintain links between customer records. For CRM to achieve its purpose, "relationship" must be about the way people are connected. Here is where the rubber meets the road with CRM. If customer relationship strategies are not about the "relationship" and the activities and interactions that forge human relationships, then all you are doing is collect names of people that will eventually go buy from your competitor. Relationships are not about databases or impersonal transactions; they are about people. The fact that they are "business" relationships does not change what a relationship is.

Tim Sanders, former Chief Solution Officer at Yahoo, brought this to light in his book "Love Is the Killer App."[12] Tim uses terms like "love-cat" to describe people whose willingness to share information and insight are based on generosity and genuine desire to help others through more meaningful relationships. The book is filled with concepts that, like the word relationship, sometimes make business people uncomfortable: terms like giving, generosity, sharing, compassion, and even love. The business climate is changing to become more receptive to the idea that we are building "personal" relationships through processes compatible with the ways we build personal relationships outside of work. Extrication of the word "relationship" from the terms "customer" or "client" or "employee" or "partner" is like removing its soul.

Unfortunately you face the reality of a workplace where CRM is about "technology" rather than "people" and the processes that help you gain their loyalty. Technology companies have driven what CRM is and what it means for far too long, and we have allowed it in exchange for quick fixes that in the end because even bigger investments. We opted to implement tools that, while very cool, were never intended to replace our efforts to cultivate relationships, but rather to automate processes that gave us more time to do so. Cultivating relationships, you see, requires labor, care, and even study. CRM tools were meant to give us more time to listen to customers, improve their experiences, make them feel good about how well we addressed their expectations.

THE A, B, Cs... AND D AND E OF RELATIONSHIPS

Relationship building is decisive. It prompts us to ask questions like, "With whom do I want to build a meaningful relationship?", and "What interactions lead to a stronger relationship?" Interpersonal relationships are interesting to study, to say the least, and there are people who dedicate their life to analyzing how we establish both the brief and enduring relationships within our personal and business lives. This chapter is not an in-depth study of human psychology, but does compel you to think about the nature of relationships and the similarities between how we establish them, nourish them, and even end them.

What if I told you that in twenty-three years of marriage neither my wife Shelley nor I have ever done anything meaningful or intentional to keep our relationship alive? Or that we simply met one day and, without any formulated ideas about what we wanted in a relationship decided just to get married? Would you believe me? Would you in the least suspect that there was something wrong with the relationship if I asserted that no effort was ever put into it since we said, "I do" yet it was thriving? What if I added that through happy times, hardships, ups and downs, and five children together, we never made any investments into the relationship after reciting our marriage vows? Surely, you would wonder if I am telling you the whole story.

The truth is that I knew the qualities I wanted in a mate ever since I was a teenager (so did my wife ...and lucky me I was a close resemblance). That is the case with most people who want to have a meaningful relationship with another. You know what you want from a relationship and the more significant the relationship, the more time you spend listening, reading, and asking people about how to improve it. As a father of five and grandfather of two, I spend a lot of time evaluating how much time I should spend with each, always mindful that they all have different needs and expectations. Relationships take special care and attention to develop and retain. They get better when we pay attention to them and they deteriorate when we do not.

Why then, would you expect to have a good relationship with customers without doing anything to understand how they prefer to do business with you, or if they consider their experiences with you worth telling others about? Why is it so common for companies to sell a product to a customer with such fervor, but then not speak to them again unless they are trying to upsell them? Business relationships are based on interpersonal relationships and therefore follow similar (often identical) patterns of formation and growth. CRM strategies will never, on their own, correct bad behavior. In fact, if you do not first identify the relationships your business should nurture, CRM could potentially keep you busy focusing on the relationships that will drain your resources and budget. We build processes for sending them literature, tracking their issues, managing their information, and tracking their orders, but overlook that relationships have a process that we should manage with equal skill.

In their book, "Close Relationships: Perspectives on the Meaning of Intimacy"[13], George Levinger and Harold L. Raush explain that personal relationships can go through stages and follow natural processes towards growth or deterioration. They explain how relationships, which begin with mutual attraction or interest, display some predictable patterns.

Using the ABCDE mnemonic Levinger and Raush explain in a theoretical, but logical, manner the phases relationships go through.

- In the "acquaintance" stage, a couple may be in contact purely because of a mutual attraction or interest.

- In the "build-up" phase, parties engage in self-disclosure and become increasingly interdependent.

- In the "continuation" stage, lives become enmeshed and the relationship becomes consolidated.

- In the "deterioration" phase, the relationship may deteriorate due to an imbalance of costs and rewards, or a high number of risk factors.

- In the "end" stage, the relationship reaches deterioration that may lead the parties to end the relationship.

We know that there is a marked difference between business and personal relationships. We define a business relationship as "an association between individuals or companies entered into for commercial purposes and sometimes formalized with legal contracts or agreements."[14] We say business relationships bind us only through the contracts we forge with one another. Personal relationships are bound similarly by covenants we make with one another. Both personal and business relationships are based on trust. Both are cultivated through mutual accountability. Either can deteriorate when we do not keep our agreements. So, while the nature of the agreements we make with one another in personal and business relationships differs, how we build relationships is very similar. In fact, business relationships follow a pattern almost identical to the personal relationship stages presented by Levinger and Raush.

Given the similarities between the way interpersonal and business relationships emerge, it is also no surprise that generational differences are influencing what we call "relationship" and how we go about managing it. Not too long ago, Western culture followed a very rigid format for introducing young people in hopes the two families would grow. Traditionally it would begin with a very public meeting between families and would follow very specific steps from courtship to marriage. Taking shortcuts and jumping right into marriage or eloping was discouraged. Similarly, businesses have followed a linear process of identifying potential customers, bringing them into their customer relationship management process, and transitioning them methodically through sales process phases. We see these phases, still, deeply embedded into CRM tools. While it is true that businesses need a structured way to qualify potential customers, manage opportunities, sell products, and service those products, it is no longer true that all these things happen in a linear way. Neither does modern relationship-building. People meet online and fall in love without ever meeting in person. People learn about you and buy your products without ever speaking to someone in your company. The lack of face-to-face interaction does not change the fact that this is still a relationship, albeit of a less traditional type. What has changed is that people in both personal and business life are leveraging technology (greatly influenced by social and generational influences) to define how they want to engage (and expecting you proactively to figure out where and how).

You have to start looking at your business relationships as relationships; not connections or sales or contacts. You have to engage at the relationship level because, only when you do, will you be able adequately to manage the interactions and experiences that create emotional connections (what we now know truly keeps customers coming back). When you engage from the "relationship," you are better-prepared to address the issues more important to that stage of the relationship and can influence the outcome. Like in personal relationships, you have to learn what it takes to build a relationship or keep it from deteriorating at "that" stage and within the expectations and agreements of that stage. As a father of five, I have learned that it takes a lot of work to understand kids. I have read dozens of books on parenting and have even attended a course or two on being a better parent. That's because the parent-child relationship has specific nuances and expectations which vary depending on the stage of the relationship. Our relationships with significant others (platonic and romantic), our relationships with parents, siblings, and friends all require similar focus and skill. Customer relationships also do, and it is time we begin seeing them as what they are and learn skillfully to manage them.

Business relationships have various stages and CRM strategies and tools must effectively manage each phase, and the interactions that lead to positive customer experiences:

MAKING THEIR ACQUAINTANCE

We replace the "acquaintance" phase with words like "suspect, prospect, and lead." In this stage, the relationship is dependent on things like previous direct or indirect contact or mutual needs and interests. Leads often become business prospects, or business connections we leverage to win or keep customers. Leads can become references, mouthpieces with which you maintain an indefinite acquaintance relationship. Leads can progress to become customers, partners, or employees. The difficulty in identifying someone as a "lead" (complicated by the very term "lead" itself) is that we often approach a relationship with people with the interest of it "leading" somewhere (thus the term). Saying that we are only interested in meeting someone to see where it "leads" may sound a bit shallow in a personal relationship, but within a business setting where we are investing time and money to better serve our customers, employees, and partners, this is the most important first step in CRM.

In other words, you and your company must decide in which relationships to invest. You are assessing not only which relationships present an opportunity to close a sale, but which relationships you will commit to and invest. Any business lead that does not qualify as a relationship in which you can and will invest time is bound for disappointment from the start. I come from a very conservative background in which boys are expected to court girls before considering marriage. My dad was adamant about me only dating girls I would consider marrying. As I got older, I deviated (significantly) from that goal and learned exactly why that was such a brilliant advice. It is exhausting to spend so much emotional capital in a relationship that leads nowhere. A lead is the speed-date of the business relationship, and it is at this phase that we quantify the type of relationship it will become and the level of investment we are going to make to pursue, maintain, or end it.

You may find the comparison of lead to a potential romantic partner humorous, but Tom Searcy, author of "RFPs Suck! How to Master the RFP System Once and for All" [15] suggests that:

"When a prospect calls, your objective should be to start dancing and see if it leads to romance."

Courtship is expensive, and when you are running a business, you have to spend wisely, evaluating the potential for a relationship to yield fruit. Some companies have strict policies in place that require salespeople to present their case and show evidence that there is a real opportunity in the mix before approving a "pursuit" budget with discretionary funds to pursue a relationship. While being a good steward of company funds is always good and necessary, you should also consider that every relationship leaves an impression. You do not want to leave a path of broken hearts and angry potentials behind. Social media is both generous and unforgiving. It gets the word out about the positive things you do, and spreads like wildfire when you create a bad experience. CRM applications provide a great advantage in this area by allowing you to keep information segregated from active sales activity, but connected to the interactions you had with non-customers. Features that link the relationship that exists between leads, partners, colleagues, and employees are extremely useful in discovering the relationships you have built (or someone else may have damaged) so you can take action to maintain or repair them.

TRANSPARENCY AND SELF-DISCLOSURE

As with personal relationships, business relationships grow when we are open and transparent with customer and create an environment that promotes and earns their transparency. Trust opens revolving doors for self-disclosure, which must be a primary goal in any CRM process. The need for transparency and self-disclosure, and business relationships that become increasingly interdependent was inescapable. Author Dennis DeGregor ("The Customer-Transparent Enterprise") poses this question as he elaborates on the need for customer transparency:

"The development of the Customer-Transparent business model came about from asking ourselves the following question: In a rapidly changing 21st century technology environment, where the customer has 24x7x365 access to information and SS&M processes through an ever-increasing array of distribution channels, and where the customer increasingly 'sells themselves' and demands a self-designed experience, what is the impact of this evolving customer behavior on corporate productivity?" [16]

Transparency and self-disclosure are important because they allow us to go directly to the need and openly discuss ways to meet it through mutual conversation and collaboration. Because CRM manages more than relationships with customers, consider the following benefits of transparency and self-disclosure across all of your business relationships:

- With customer and partner relationships: Facilitates strategic and solution-driven conversations that result in real value to your business.

- Within customer interactions: Enables you to explore better ways to serve and correct mistakes of the past.

- Within employee relationships: Transparency and self-disclosure allows you to share company-wide vision and win the commitment of people as contributors and champions. It also allows you to listen to honest feedback about the way current initiatives are affecting people personally and professionally. Remember, you have to take care of the people who are rewarding the customer for doing business with you.

CRM is, once again a great vehicle for driving the businesses processes that promote and solicit transparency from your customers, but it must be integrated with all the efforts that collect honest customer feedback. CRM cannot limit feedback to the perception of the people interacting with customers by asking them how they thought the interaction went. Way too often CRM becomes an obstacle to progress when companies base customer perception on shallow information: usually from drop-down options asking if the customer was "satisfied" after a call. There are great instruments you should incorporate into CRM to gain a balanced perspective of customer sentiment. Ask about how your company is using Net Promoter Score (NPS) to determine which of your customers are promoting your products and services. Dig into where Cx Index measurements are collected and tracked. Use

CRM to collect and centralize information from customer surveys (word of mouth, voice of the employee, voice of the customer, etc.).

CONTINUATION THROUGH RELATIONSHIP CARE

You should aim to reach this stage as a natural result of building relationships based on self-disclosure and trust. Here relationships become more consolidated and open. Anyone who has been in a relationship for a long time knows the importance of this stage. In this stage if the customer sees the grass greener on the other side, then it is time for you to water your lawn and fix your fence. As with personal relationships, business relationships require you make the necessary investments to keep it healthy.

The continuation stage is where we get to balance the perception of costs and rewards, and can reduce risks to the relationship. Here is where we show people that we are not only interested in winning them, but keeping them and rewarding them for their commitment to the relationship.

DETERIORATION

Not all relationships deteriorate, but when they do, there are always signs that the relationship is in trouble. Sadly, over-dependence on technology to remind you of when you should be talking to a customer can keep you from seeing the relationship deteriorate as it happens. Salespeople experience this when they wait for an automated email to remind them that a customer's yearly maintenance is due, only to realize during the call or visit to the client that, to their embarrassment, the customer is about to leave him for a competitor.

Dissatisfaction and resentment are not reserved to personal relationships. They happen in business and cause people to communicate less and avoid self-disclosure. They also cause people to lose trust in you and your company and ultimately send the relationship into a sometimes-irreparable state that leads to the end of the relationship.

ENDING

Business relationships can end with as much heartache and drama as a personal relationship. Both can result in hurt feelings and a range of emotions (from relief to anger). When business relationships end because both parties understand that they are better apart than together, the breakup can be easier to accept. When business relationships meet a bitter end, the damage (both emotional and financial) can be as bad as a divorce. In cases where it is you or your company that has violated the customer's trust (or the trust of someone within your company) the following advice from the Mayo Clinic on mending a broken marriage is both applicable, sobering, and worthy of incorporating into the CRM practices of your organization:

• BE ACCOUNTABLE. Take responsibility for your actions. End the behavior that caused the loss of trust immediately. Be honest. Once the initial shock is over, discuss what happened openly and honestly — no matter how difficult talking or hearing about the problem may be.

• CONSIDER SHARED GOALS. It may take time to sort out what has happened and to consider whether your relationship can heal. If you share a goal of reconciliation, realize that recovering trust will take time, energy, and commitment.

• CONSULT A THIRD PARTY trained in the issue that caused the problem. Third parties such as conflict mediators can help you put the situation in perspective, identify issues that may have contributed to it, help you learn how to rebuild and strengthen the relationship, and avoid ending it.

• MAKE EVERY EFFORT TO RESTORE TRUST at any cost, even if the relationship will end or has ended anyway.

As with personal relationships outside of work, there are many myths and misunderstandings about what it takes to maintain a relationship healthy and growing. We bring some of these myths with us to the workplace and subsequently incorporate them into our business processes. Most common among them are the following misconceptions about relationship-building:

• Relationships that appear to be healthy do not require work. You have heard the expression that relationships are like gardens that need care and cultivation to stay healthy. This analogy is as true about customer relationships as it is about personal relationships. Strong, enduring relationships between people require proactive focus.

- If you have a good relationship, you should be able to anticipate what the other person needs and feels. This one is tricky. While it is true that the better you know a person or company the better you will be able to provide for their needs and proactively cater to them, you have to be careful to base your efforts on facts and not conjecture. If you do not think consumers expect you to be proactive in knowing what they need, take note of the relationship Apple has with their Macheads, or ACT! with their ACT! Fanatics. Both groups look with anticipation for these companies to understand them and anticipate their needs. CRM strategies require that you take into account the feelings and expectations people have about you and the feelings and expectations they communicate to you and one another.

- Conflict ruins relationships. Companies avoid conflict with customers and in the process miss the opportunity to resolve problems. Conflicts do not ruin relationships. Failure to resolve conflict ruins relationships.

- In order for a relationship to be successful, the other person must change. This advice goes against the better judgment of the "customer is always right" attitude championed by Harry Gordon Selfridge (1857-1947) founder of London's Selfridges department store. What he (and other 20th-century companies like Marshall Field's) was trying to institute was the idea that we should treat the customer as if they were right, even when they were not. This is a mental attitude that stimulates empathy and opens a dialog that leads to a better understanding of customer needs. The customer already expects you to give them the benefit of the doubt. Therefore, your CRM business processes must align with this expectation.

Like with all human associations, it takes a conscious, concentrated effort to maintain a healthy relationship. The five stages originally proposed by Dr. Levinger are purely theoretical and logical. It is difficult to see when or where one crosses the boundary between one phase and another. Therefore, it is important to emphasize the idea of transitions among the phases. Sometimes acquaintanceships lead to the third phase without progressing through the stages. The model is primarily a rhetorical device and not truly amenable to "research." However, it helps us to visualize how relationships can progress.

Perhaps the most interesting aspect of the similarities between personal and business relationships is that the ultimate decision for continuing or ending is based on an emotional connection. We are, after all, human beings driven to decisions based on both facts and feelings. Referenced earlier, the Customer Experience Index identified by Forester Research clearly credits a customer's willingness to consider you for another purchase, likelihood to recommend you, and the likelihood to switch to a competitor on how they rate their experiences with you. Customers, at each interaction with you, are measuring the experience to determine if they accomplished their goal, if you made it easy, and if, as a result, they felt good about it. But while the alignment of customer experience with customer behavior (and its application to customer strategy) is truly brilliant, it is not new. It is also incomplete unless we learn to assess experiences within the framework of the relationship phases it may go through. Experiences are not independent of relationships and vice versa. It is within the relationship framework, the phase it is undergoing, and the expectations of that stage that people make value assessments (imbalance in cost, rewards, and risk) to either continue or end the relationship. Experiences build relationships, and relationships define the right experiences to deliver.

The quality of your business, like the quality of your life, is measured by the quality of your relationships. Before you create measurement mechanisms and metrics of your sales pipeline, be sure to measure the quality of your relationships.

ARTICLE 6

POWER TO THE INTERACTION

WE WILL CREATE BUSINESS PROCESSES THAT MAKE OUR INTERACTIONS WITH PEOPLE INTENTIONAL. WE WILL BE MINDFUL OF THE IMPACT OUR INTERACTIONS HAVE IN THE LIVES OF PEOPLE AND THE LIFE OF OUR BUSINESS.

```
man·age verb \'ma-nij\: to handle or
direct with a degree of skill¹⁷
```

"Happiness is not something ready made. It comes from your own actions." - Dalai Lama

Understanding that customer relationships follow the same patterns of growth and deterioration as other relationships compels us to make our interactions with customers, and the experiences that result from them, intentional and meaningful. We are connected to customers in a relationship that, to be successful, must be reciprocal. It must offer a benefit to both parties for the relationship to be equitable. We manage that reciprocal process during each interaction with customers. The idea that we must "manage" our interactions with people has negative connotations for some who associate the word with oppressive practices in the workplace. In spite of that, the word "manage" really is the perfect word to use when talking about customer relationship practices. There are many definitions for the word "manage"; the most applicable to CRM being this one from the Merriam-Webster dictionary:

"To handle or direct with a degree of skill"

It applies because the "management" aspect of "customer

relationship management" is about skillfully handling (requiring capability) and skillfully directing (requiring intentional strategy) how we handle our customer relationships. Interacting with customers (regardless of communication channel) takes skill. It takes skill to identify interactions that need care and cultivate the ones that are going well. It takes skill to build strategies that incorporate client preferences for interacting with you. It takes skills to listen, learn, and act on the interactions people are having on social media, community forums, events, and anywhere they interact with your company, your partners, and other customers. It takes skill to create processes that guide interactions in the right direction.

Great customer interactions are the result of objective and persistent alignment between the interaction and the relationship, in perspective with where the relationship is and in support of all the other customer strategies that support the customer. A phone interaction is never "just" a call. That call is part of a relationship journey that started with the identification of the customer as a good fit. It came about because someone at your company established the right engagement channels and even a customized experience for them. It is supported by customer service and support agreements that set guidance for how you treat them and what to do when you don't meet their expectations. It is part of your company's strategy to present a single, transparent brand to your customer. It is one of many steps you take emotionally to connect your customer to your company through great customer experiences. What you perceive as just a phone call may connect your company's relationship, engagement, centricity, service, transparency, and experience strategies for that customer.

It is important to recognize that some companies view "customer interaction management" (CIM) as a completely separate competency managed by contact center systems. It is, for some companies, disconnected from the interactions (or activities) that CRM systems manage. Perhaps because many of the channels used to interact with customers are managed by call center solutions and the responsibility of call center / contact center teams. However, as a strategy for understanding the customer intimately and predicting the best ways to interact with them, customer interaction management is an integral part of CRM. Customer interaction management strategies help us build a detailed picture of the customer in order to predict their behavior and create tailored experiences. The interactions that call center systems manage and the history of customer interactions managed in CRM systems, together, help us accomplish that goal.

INTERACTIONS AND THE CUSTOMER EXPERIENCE

Just as CRM initiatives fail because they did not meet the expectations of the people executing the strategy and using the technology, interactions with customers fail to accomplish their intended purpose when you disconnect them from the experience it is intended to create. Relationships are the affiliations, associations, and connections we have with customers. Customer experiences are what customers use to determine if they want that relationship to grow or end. Interactions are the moments of opportunity you use to create positive customer experiences.

For years, Forester Research has been writing "The Business Impact of Customer Experience" report to help maintain focus on the importance of Customer Experience as a unique competency. This year (as part of an online Q4 2013 survey of 7,506 US consumers about their interactions with 154 large US brands in a range of different industries) Forrester again found a parallel between how customers rate their experience with a company and their subsequent choices to remain loyal. Forrester uses a measure called the "Customer Experience Index" (CXi) which uses three models to estimate the impact customer experience has on three loyalty measures:

- willingness to consider the company for another purchase

- likelihood to switch business

- and likelihood to recommend

The study shows that "the strong correlation between CXi and loyalty means that companies with higher CXi scores tend to have more customers who will buy from them again, who won't take their business elsewhere, and who will recommend them to a friend." Managing the customer experience builds customer relationships, but also directly impacts revenue from customers who stay with you and bring in new customers.

There is a notable difference between a server who asks if

there is "anything else you need", and the one who asks, "How does your food taste?" The first, while friendly, is approaching you as a transaction. Asking you what you need is part of several interactions you will have with her over the course of the meal. The "taste" question is about the experience of enjoying your food. It aims to reconcile the experience you expected with the one they are creating for you. Restaurants often tell you that they want you to have an enjoyable "dining experience." That's because for all practical purposes you could have gone through the Burger King drive-through or re-heated last night's dinner at home. The "experience" is why you are there. Other companies will aim for you to have a great "shopping experience" or a pleasant "travel experience." Companies that design customer interactions as channels to great customer experiences understand what customer relationship management is about.

It is what marketing firms like J. D. Power rate when awarding a company a "Highest in Customer Satisfaction Award," an accolade companies like GMC promote as a highly ranked customer experience endorsement. This year GMC received the highest numerical score among mass-market brands in the J.D. Power and Associates Customer Satisfaction with Dealer Service (CSI) Study. The results are based on responses from 91,723 owners and lessees of 2008 to 2012 model-year vehicles, measuring 32 auto manufacturers and measures satisfaction among vehicle owners who visit a dealer for service during the first three years of ownership. Proprietary study results are based on experiences and perceptions of owners surveyed from October-December 2012. The J. D. Power website reads:

"Getting the right information depends on asking, listening, and watching. Of course, asking is the easy part, and is what most survey research is designed to do. But it is not enough to simply ask what customers think about your brand or how satisfied they are with your products or services. You also need to listen to what they say and watch what they do."

Customer Relationship Management drives the business processes that enable customer interactions as well as the processes that evaluate and survey the quality of customer experiences. To disconnect the interaction from the experience is myopic and the reason so many people think that Customer Experience Management is disconnected from CRM (and that it is a new strategy designed to supersede CRM). Managing customer experience is a logical function of CRM tools and necessary part of any CRM strategy. For the strategy to be effective, you have to make customer interactions intentional and customer experiences memorable, from the customer's perspective.

CHANNELS: SUPPORTING THE LONG DISTANCE RELATIONSHIPS

For the past few years, I have been fortunate to work from my home office. My wife, who has her own home-based business, works upstairs from our master bedroom while I work from my office in the basement. Our proximity to one another allows us to go to lunch together frequently.

When Shelley needs something from me all she has to do is give a shout, and I respond. Occasionally we rely on text messages for communications requiring a quick response, but most of the time we speak face to face. Working from home is great, and I am one of the lucky few who get to do it these days. However, when I travel, Shelley and I have to get creative with how we communicate. Geography, business hours, time zones, and availability of phone reception and internet access dictate the channels we use to stay in contact, solve problems, or share information. When circumstances are ideal, we both have preferred interaction channels depending on where we are and what we are doing. Couples who are away for extended periods of time (and the now more common) long-distance relationship, demand that the ways we communicate with one another more efficient, accessible, and in alignment with our lifestyles. If a particular channel is available to one person, the other will wonder why their significant other isn't using it to help keep the relationship alive.

As we emphasize that customer relationships are like other human relationships, we begin to see a pattern emerge, especially between customer relationships and long-distance relationships. You could even say that, for the most part, customer relationships ARE long-distance relationships. Except for companies that enjoy frequent face-to-face interactions with customers (retail stores, hotels, restaurants, etc.), most of our interactions with customers are conducted via channels that do not require a person to be physically present. As with the previous analogy about long-distance relationships, customers know what interaction channels are available and expect you to make them available to keep the relationship alive.

How people interact with one another has changed over time. When CRM systems first came into the corporate marketplace (and for many years since) they recorded interactions that took place via:

• In person

• Email

• Phone

• Mail (now snail mail)

As communication technology evolves, we make adjustments to make sure CRM tools record those interactions adequately. Customer interactions can now include interactions that occur via:

• Web portals

• Kiosks

• Mobile device

• Messaging

• Text or video chat

However, relationship building isn't just about the interactions you have directly with customers, but also about the interactions they have with one another. When these interactions take place via social media, they may be between your customer and someone with whom you are not even connected. Here is where our relationship comparison gets interesting. Here is where we have to return to what a relationship is and how people behave to create or maintain it. Take this scenario for example:

You are having coffee at your local coffee house and overhear two people talking. From their conversation, you realize that one of them is a customer of your company. The customer is telling his coffee buddy that he recently had a very negative experience with your company and that they were considering purchasing from the competition the next time they needed services. Do you take the opportunity to offer the customer help? Is the customers expectation that you should jump in to offer assistance since you overheard the need? Or would they find it intrusive that you initiated an interaction at an external forum? Even if it is a public place. What if the person was not your customer and you overheard them say that they were in the market for a new vehicle; one that your car dealership sells? Does the message that there is intent to buy, once again delivered in a public forum, make it acceptable to engage this person?

These scenarios are just as common in the coffee house as they are on social media and you will have to decide how to manage them. Social interactions are just that; interactions that happen in social media. The decision to engage in the interaction follows the same rules as when we deal with the same conversations in person. The advent of social media does not create a need for a new type of "Social CRM." It simply requires that CRM strategies take into account that there is yet another channel where customer interactions happen. What is true, however, is that CRM tools have had to evolve to allow you to manage social conversations within the CRM record itself. Like with the inclusion of chat into our customer interaction channels, CRM tools must incorporate social conversation feeds and make them part of the 360-degree perspective of the customer. Remember that, like social media today, chat was the hot technology we added to our list of customer interaction channels.

Technology will bring many more innovative channels you will be able to use to communicate with your customers. What is important is that you treat channels as the bridge you are building to help the customer interact with you. Sometimes it is a bridge that guides them to where they need to go to help themselves. Sometimes it is a bridge that brings them to the best place for you to help them. Sometimes it requires that you build a bridge to where they are. The better scenario is that you allow the customer multiple channels to interact with you. The best scenario is that they are able to transition seamlessly from one channel to another, based on their needs, without feeling like the channels are disconnected or part of a single experience. The idea of "multi-channel" speaks to the customers' ability to reach you in many ways (preferably ways you have identified as most beneficial to them). While "omni-channel" refers to the customer's perception of experiencing those channels as a seamless, unified journey between them.

CRITICAL POINTS OF INTERACTION

During a conference in New York last year I was asked, as part of a panel of customer executives, to help answer the question "what do customers really want?". I believe my response was, "thank you for asking me a question only more difficult to answer than 'what do women really want?'. After the audience had stopped laughing, I continued to explain that as a young incredulous boy I thought I understood girls my age only to realize the magnificent complexity of the opposite sex. I also thought I understood women as I started dating, and then after I got married; becoming increasingly knowledgeable as I endeavored to have a great relationship with my wife. Then, just as I thought I had it figured out, I had daughters. Then a granddaughter. Each of my daughters is different and responds differently to different situations. Their age, environment, emotional state, perceptions, and expectations change the scenario and compel me to make decisions based on many, constantly changing, factors affecting the relationship. Some days it feels like there are no consistent patterns of behavior until I stand back and studiously evaluate each event. Then I begin to see patterns and what I call "critical points of interaction."

While there are distinct types of interactions that help qualify prospects, sell a product, or follow up on a complaint, there are particular interaction that can make or break a relationship. They are "critical" because they could result in abrupt changes to your relationships and must be managed with the highest sense of urgency. In this context, the definition of "manage" (to handle or direct with a degree of skill) is even more relevant. Managing is about conscious direction. Applied to relationships, "managing" means treating something with care. It is synonymous with the ideas of leading, caring, negotiating, and overseeing. You must manage critical interactions with surgical precision, acknowledging that they are especially significant to the growth or deterioration of your customer relationships. Psychologist tell us that there are times in our personal relationship when a single event can change the direction of the relationship. Among them are the first use of the word "we", the first fight, discussions about the future, and talks about commitment. They are interactions that turn into defining moments. That is what critical interactions are to customer relationships.

In his book "How to Win Customers and Keep Them for Life"[18] Dr. Michael LeBoeuf encourages us to be mindful of what he calls the "moments of truth," those crucial points of customer contact when you have the opportunity to share your value proposition and show genuine customer care. I would like to draw from his list and isolate the most critical interactions CRM must manage with extra emphasis:

INTERACTIONS WITH ANGRY OR DEFENSIVE PEOPLE

Not to overstate the obvious, but anger and defensiveness are warning bells that alert you that something is amiss in your relationship with someone. The range of emotions anger provokes can stem from a number of issues. Guiding the conversation towards resolution is always important, even if the problem is not your fault. Between the physical reaction that both parties experience, and the behavior they exhibit, is the cognitive experience of anger.

Does the customer feel that what happened was wrong, unfair, or undeserved? Why? What were the events that brought it to pass? Armed with those answers you will be better prepared to solve the problem. Of all the things we manage poorly in CRM, anger and defensiveness rank highest. Returning anger and defensiveness with more anger and defensiveness never ends well. Remember, this is about relationship management, so you must engage people with the mindset that you want to help build the relationship (and yes, that takes skill). Deal first with people's feelings, and then help them with the problem that is making them angry.

Build a CRM strategy that gives people resources for managing this type of interaction effectively. Build a strong workflow and resources in your CRM tool that help organize contact history in a way you can leverage it during your interaction.

INTERACTIONS WHERE A SPECIAL REQUEST IS MADE

Special requests are sometimes a manifestation of something missing or incomplete in what you delivered to the customer. Managing interactions that involve a special request can turn crisis into a successful collaboration with people whose expectations have not been met. That is because special request discussions allow us to listen to what customers want in relation to what they got (and that is always a good thing).

CRM interactions like special requests are critical because they can branch off into other profitable interactions for your company:

1. SERVICE OPPORTUNITY – We seldom get an opportunity to show people how much we really care about them, but when we respond positively to a need, it shows that we are willing to be flexible.

2. ASSESSMENT OPPORTUNITY – When someone explains a need or special request it opens doors for questions about how you have done the job to-date.

3. PROMOTIONAL OPPORTUNITY – One can never underestimate the importance of self-promotion. Most people do not realize the value of the products and services you provide until you tell them. Here is your chance.

4. BUSINESS OPPORTUNITY – It angers me when I am in a project and one of my teammates gets upset because the customer asks for more than what we originally agreed to do for them. A change request or request for customization should never represent an inconvenience. It should represent an opportunity for new and repeat business.

5. COMPETITIVE ADVANTAGE – Needless to say, if you are always willing to cater to the special needs of people, your competition is going to have a hard time catching up.

INTERACTIONS WHERE THE CUSTOMER CAN'T MAKE UP HIS MIND

When people waver between two or more possible courses of action, they need someone to help guide the way. Indecision provides an opportunity to move people through stages in the relationship. In CRM, we identify not only where people are in their relationship with us, but also who can make decisions about strengthening that relationship. Indecision can be a clear sign that you are not talking to the person that can best nurture the relationship.

Indecision may indicate that the person you identified in your sales cycle as the "decision-maker" may be the wrong person.

To a sales person this significant mistake could misdirect them to invest valuable time in efforts that do not lead to growing the relationship or closing the sale. It could mean that while your company is talking to the person you think is responsible for choosing you, the right person may be elsewhere talking to your competition.

Indecision is not only bad for you, but also bad for your customer. Every minute of indecision could constitute a delay in delivering something of value. This middle of the road behavior could be a cry for help from people who need you but do not know how to ask. In either case, staying in the middle of the road is never good.

"Indecision is debilitating; it feeds upon itself; it is, one might almost say, habit-forming. Not only that, but it is contagious; it transmits itself to others. . . . Business is dependent upon action. It cannot go forward by hesitation. Those in executive positions must fortify themselves with facts and accept responsibility for decisions based upon them. Often greater risk is involved in postponement than in making a wrong decision." – H. A. Hopf

It falls on us sometimes to move people off the road for their own good by recommending options that help manage the relationship and lead it towards a mutually beneficial choice.

INTERACTIONS THAT RAISE OBJECTIONS OR OBSTACLES

It is amazing what people will tell you when you are truly listening. A person will tell you they do not want to buy and some people will only hear rejection. However, if you are listening, truly listening, you will see obstacles to remove and objections to address instead.

This is another good instance of people opening doors for you to make your case. What most people are telling you when they present objections is that they do not see the value of what you are selling. No CRM strategy is more effective than a well-prepared, knowledgeable human being who expertly deals with objections. However, CRM tools can serve as a knowledge repository companies can leverage to maintain value proposition information essential to addressing product and service value. Used correctly, a CRM tool (properly positioned by a well-thought-out CRM strategy) can serve as a knowledge resource immediately available during these interactions.

INTERACTIONS THAT REVEAL INTEREST IN BUYING

Interactions where people tell you they want to buy are happy moments in the life of a company. Unfortunately, not everyone who interacts with the customer gets the hint.

As the father of five, three of which are grown adults, I have lots of experience with a humorous phenomenon related to teenage kids. I call it romantic cluelessness. Around the time they start liking the opposite sex and inviting them to dinner at our house, they also start to miss the obvious. Once their visitor leaves I ask them, "how long has that girl (or boy) liked you?" Their reaction is like that of spraying a cat with a water bottle (matching facial expressions and all). Sometimes you get very clear hints that someone likes you and miss it completely.

CRM is a strategy that guides people to the right channels and processes when someone wants to buy. However, you first have to be receptive to buying signals. Once you do that it becomes easier to follow the right CRM process to route the opportunity.

There are more interactions affecting the way you build relationships with people in business. Delivering bad news, responding to complaints, and delivering information about a product or service a customer got from you are some of them. They all present opportunities to gain trust, and reward people with positive action. But critical interactions, faithfully managed, can save your business. Every interaction, every activity, and every action you take to build relationships results in the development or restoration of trust.

ARTICLE 7

POWER TO THE CUSTOMER

WE WILL MAKE THE CUSTOMER'S
PERCEPTION OF SUCCESS OUR
MEASURE FOR CRM SUCCESS.

```
ser·vice noun \'sər-vəs\: contribution
to the welfare of others¹⁹
```

"Life's most urgent question is: What are you doing for others?" - Martin Luther King, Jr.

Managing critical interactions is a natural part of building relationships with people. All relationships require meaningful interactions to survive. Any relationship worth keeping requires emotional investment and that all parties are willing to be vulnerable and exposed in order to bring issues to resolution. This proposition feels risky to some, but building relationships is about human interaction, and human beings make decisions based on their perception of the health of the relationship, not yours.

Any CRM effort that helps you build relationships and manage them, but then measures its success on your own perception of its success is myopic and narrow-minded. That's because the only person that matters when it comes to rating the strength of the relationship is the customer. We are all faithful servants of the people we serve, and servants do not give themselves rate cards over their performance. After your teams commit to collaborate in the grand effort we call CRM, and agree to focus on relationship building, the only way to measure if you were successful is for your customers to say so.

This is why the CRM industry has such a bad reputation. We formulate strategies and purchase expensive tools to deploy them, but neglect evaluating if any of that investment improved the customer's perception of the quality of our service. This is an idea fully explored by Peter Hernon and Danuta Nitecki in their study of service quality (Service Quality: A Concept Not Fully Explored) at Texas A&M University. The researchers noted that most businesses have an externally imposed requirement to implement service quality principles; an imposition made by customers who expect them to be accountable and compete for their loyalty. Customers who share information about their expectations offer an opportunity for the company to establish a closer personal contact with them. The study asserts, "Fundamental to service quality is the need for cyclic review of service goals and objectives in relation to customer expectations."

Service quality has been defined from at least four perspectives:[20] Excellence, Value, Conformance, and Meeting / Exceeding Expectations. The problem with this model is that:

• EXCELLENCE - Excellence is often externally defined. It may be a worthy aim but one that changes dramatically and rapidly from person to person.

• VALUE - It incorporates multiple attributes, but quality and value are different concepts. One is the perception of meeting or exceeding expectations, and the other stresses benefit to the recipient.

- CONFORMANCE – It facilitates precise measurement, but users of a service may not know or care about internal specifications.

- MEETING OR EXCEEDING EXPECTATIONS. This definition is all encompassing and applies across service industries, but expectations change and may be shaped by experiences with other service providers.

According to the study, what customers are looking for is, in fact, simple: they are looking for a confirmation or disconfirmation of their perceptions. Customers rate this perception on five interrelated dimensions that they most value when they evaluate service quality:

1. TANGIBLES – the appearance of physical facilities, equipment, personnel, and communication material

2. RELIABILITY – the ability to perform the promised service dependably and accurately

3. RESPONSIVENESS – the willingness to help customers and provide prompt service

4. EMPATHY – the caring, individualized attention that a firm provides its customers

5. ASSURANCE – the knowledge and courtesy of employees and their ability to inspire trust and confidence

Any strategy or technology that aims to manage corporate relationships at any level must incorporate mechanisms that track against these traits and uses them as baseline for success. A more important question than how a business process will be implemented or automated is "did it increase the perception of empathy with the customer?" A better measure of the success of a newly implemented service level agreement is "did it improve perception of responsiveness."

These are qualities all members of the organization must emulate across sales, marketing, support, service, supply chain, and advocacy programs at all levels of your company (not just by management or customer-facing functions) through activities the customer will perceive. While sales and opportunity pipeline management, marketing campaign response tracking, service level maintainability, and other operational measures are needed to gage the financial health and revenue pipeline of your business, these are the ingredients that determine if you are being successful. In asking these questions, you ensure that every interaction leads to the correct perception from the customer.

IS YOUR SERVICE TANGIBLE?

Companies do not spend millions of dollars in advertising during the Super Bowl to be funny; they do so to be noticeable. Advertisement is designed to present a certain image that draws customer attention. That attention is going to engender a response. Company policies that dictate what employees wear and how they act do the same thing. That's because appearances are a tangible way for customers to see how you feel about them.

Anything the customer sees, feels, touches, hears, or smells concerning you and your company is shaping their perception of service quality. Clothing and food retailers understand this well. The slightest negative perception that an establishment is dirty could close a restaurant. That is why even when a health department favorably grades a restaurant; it can still lose business if its patrons perceive it to be unclean or unattractive. Appearances can be deceiving, but customers draw many conclusions about you based on what they see.

IS YOUR SERVICE RELIABLE?

Do people feel that you and your company can be trusted? People want you to be predictable in your patterns of behavior as much as they want to depend on you to do what you say you are going to do. People want consistent performance out of your interactions. If you want to know if you are reliable, then the following statements must be true:

- I do what I say I will do

- I do it when I say I will do it.

- I aim to do it right the first time.

- I get it done on time.

Reliability is about the consistent behavior that makes you credible in the eyes of people. Credibility is the measure of trust. When people see you as credible, they are willing to give you their trust on credit. Strong relationships require peace of mind and credibility gives people security, integrity, and the assurance that they can trust you even if someone else in the same role or position failed them. Credibility is your door to second chances, a benefit that businesses need to stay competitive.

IS YOUR SERVICE RESPONSIVE?

Being responsive means being accessible, available, and willing to help, which can translate to the time it took to respond as much as to the nature and temperament of the response. By definition, being responsive means, "responding especially, readily and sympathetically to appeals, efforts, and influences."

It is particularly applicable to CRM, which tries to appeal to specific audiences in an effort to influence their decisions through relationship building. CRM strategies and technology account for the recording of service response time, but in addition, gauging responsiveness helps you:

• Create realistic service level agreements

• Build automated processes that help people improve response time

• Measure the efforts that lead to customer satisfaction and peer collaboration

IS YOUR SERVICE EMPATHETIC?

What better use of CRM than to achieve the goal of measuring if you and your company have the right measure of empathy as perceived by customers. When you are empathetic, you are experiencing the feelings, thoughts, and attitudes of another. CRM strategies must aim to better understand people in order to treat them as unique individuals, with their unique personality and distinctive wants and reasoning, so you can create unique experiences for them. When we step outside our own need to understand the needs of others, we experience empathy.

When we imagine their problems and walk through them in our minds to help resolve them, we experience empathy. We can express empathy sometimes without saying a word. And because our goal is to build genuine relationships with people, sometimes that conscious empathy turns into sincere sympathy for people that motivates us to understand their distress and help alleviate it. At that moment, we come to the transcendent understanding that compassion does not have to be reserved for our personal relationships.

DOES YOUR SERVICE INSPIRE TRUST?

A customer's perception of service through their assessment of how reliable, responsive, and empathetic you are, is helping them build an inevitable conclusion about you. Do they, or do they not, trust you. Trust may be the single most important ingredient for the development and maintenance of happy, well-functioning relationships. Several major theories, including attachment theory (Bowlby, 1969) and Erikson's (1963) theory of psychosocial development, are built on the premise that higher levels of trust in relationships early in life lay the psychological foundation for happier and better functioning relationships in adulthood. It is therefore reasonable to expect that every effort to build business relationships must lead towards building trust.

Customers watch your behavior and ask, although not usually verbally: "Can I trust this person? Can I trust this company?" They want the assurance that they can put their confidence in you and rely in your honesty, dependability, and strength of character. They want to know that you do not have to be coerced or compelled to keep your word. Customers want to have faith in your ability or word in those specific areas where you provide them with service.

ARTICLE 8

POWER TO THE INSTRUMENT

WE WILL NOT BECOME SERVANTS
TO THE TOOLS THAT POWER CRM.
WE WILL CHOOSE THE TOOLS
THAT BEST ENABLE US TO BUILD
RELATIONSHIPS AND MEASURE
OUR ABILITY TO
SERVE CUSTOMERS.

```
in·stru·ment noun \'in(t)-strə-mənt\:
a means whereby something is achieved,
performed, or furthered²¹
```

"Technology is nothing. What's important is that you have a faith in people, that they're basically good and smart, and if you give them tools, they'll do wonderful things with them." - Steve Jobs

In the 1999 science-fiction movie "Bicentennial Man," Robin Williams stars as Andrew, an android who, through his interactions with his human owners and the world around him, endeavors to become human. In his role as a computerized servant, Andrew struggles to understand the idiosyncrasies of his biological masters though sometimes humorous but always touching interactions. Andrew's mission in life is service. He ends every interaction with others with the phrase, "One is glad to be of service"; an automatic, meaningless response built into his subroutines. But gradually, Andrew acquires emotions and the realization of the importance of relationships and heart-felt service to others that make that phrase part of his purpose in life and the message of the film.

Self-realizing technology that evolves to understand

the importance of serving customers is not available yet. But today's technology can help you become more empathetic and service-oriented. Technology cannot create the bonds required of real relationships with people, but it can facilitate the communications necessary for that bond to strengthen. Technology cannot gain the right understanding of service from customers, but it can serve as an enabling, powerful tool to the people who provide service.

The most mature CRM automation is best-known (and valued) for the way it helps organizations provide deeper service orientation, and for the way it enables its users to have more significant time with customers. It does so by also accounting for the connection a customer has to employees across the organization as well as to the vendors and partners that serve them. By definition, any technology intended to engage and maintain a relationship between people (business or personal) has at its foundation a very tangible human element to it – an element that you must reconnect with if you are going to use a CRM tool to support the practices we have discussed so far. CRM that is purely about contact record management, report generation, and other purely transactional activities, removes the "relationship" aspect at the center of CRM.

CRM technology has evolved from a contact-centric (Rolodex-type) environment to more advanced relational database systems able to connect contacts to the companies with whom they are associated, as well as to the various sales opportunities, invoices, and service tickets related to that contact. Even though not all CRM strategies require that you implement CRM technology, there are many valuable advantages to doing so:

- CRM technology is organized around the contact / account-centric model instead of products or territories. Most relational CRM applications are built on an account-centric model that allows you to see companies and contacts in relationship to one another while extending your visibility into the products and services you offer them within a geographical area or territory. The "customer" (client, citizen, constituent, or patient) remains at the center, with peripheral relationships to the people with whom they interact both inside and outside of your company

- CRM technology allows you to learn who your most profitable customers are. This practice is significant because (in most markets) 80 percent or more of the profits come from 20 percent or less of the customers. Being able to identify top customers (and what makes them so,) will make you more cognizant of the patterns that create new ones just like them. CRM applications include dashboards and list management tools that can leverage existing data to identify the very important and valuable 20 percent and the people who are nurturing those relationships.

- CRM is becoming more like people: Social. The CRM software industry is slowly moving away from mass marketing functions and is leveraging live customer intelligence (LCI) and social engagement to help users target the audience they want to reach. This activity used to be one-way (from companies to the consumer). New technology now allows us to also listen, understand, and act on what the customer really wants.

- CRM incorporates employee management tools to help you hire, train, motivate, and keep employees who take special care of the customer. Although the core functionality of CRM applications is customer-centric, it also has a foundation for the more holistic approach of maintaining all relationship data in the same system. CRM allows you to track the interaction between employee and customer, identify patterns of behavior that led to customer acquisition and retention, and even allows you to map the level and depth of relationship between the two.

- CRM manages interactions and activity history efficiently. The ability to document feedback gained through the type of discovery self-disclosure this book promotes is invaluable.

- CRM technology, using activity and process automation can remind you to engage in the interactions that cultivate relationships.

- CRM solutions include "Neglected Contacts" reports (a perfect name for what we often do to the people we call "valued customers"), and analytics that give you diagnostic, descriptive, predictive, and prescriptive insight about customers.

INVESTING IN THE RIGHT THING

In a May 2009 article, MSN Money's Michael Brush recounts a 2007 NPR interview with former Federal Reserve chairman Alan Greenspan. Among the items offered by Greenspan was the suggestion that we need look no further than our underwear drawer as an indicator of financial health. Both Brush and Greenspan argue that the proverbial and literal underwear drawer hold the key to our spending patterns. Economists agree that the sale of underwear raises and falls with the economy.

Why "knickers"? Because they are representative of a much hidden and intimate choice we make when things get tough. As Greenspan also says, "underwear is something we can hold off on buying until we really have the money."

Companies often do the same with CRM technology. What customers see gets the attention, while improvements to the internal systems used by sales, support, and marketing are put on hold. Unwittingly, companies will spend money on the very visible and attractive website, and neglect the systems that support customer relationship-building initiatives.

Female readers will note, and perhaps even argue, that women have a completely different perspective to purchasing undergarments. Most women will purchase lingerie because of the way the purchase will make them feel. Feeling stressed and want to reward yourself with something intimate and special? Buy some lingerie.

As humorous as both examples are, they accurately represent the two main reasons why companies choose to buy or not buy CRM technology, and they are both bad reasons. Investing in CRM because it will make you feel good that you are doing "something" about your immediate problems, without a clear idea of how your company will collaborate to implement it is a waste of your money.

There are important considerations to implementing CRM technology solutions. Many companies try to justify their CRM technology purchase solely on hype; not adequately evaluating the applicability to their business model or how they will implement the processes the tool is supposed to support. For example:

- Being able to connect with contacts via social media-enabled CRM tools can help you increase the number of customers you can sell to and support, but how are you leveraging this capability to build the right relationships and improve the experiences of your customers?

- Access to CRM loyalty data from portable electronic devices like tablets from within an airplane is an amazing use of modern technology. However, how should a flight attendant use it? Can she leverage it to view a passenger's travel history so she can proactively give them the best possible experience, thank them for their patronage, or rectify poor service from a previous flight? Would it negatively impact operational efficiency in-flight or improve it? How does mobile access to information help build, maintain, or restore relationships?

If I had a bad experience on my flight from Atlanta to LA, and the flight attendant from the connecting flight from LA to Sydney offered me a complementary drink for my trouble, would I find that insightful and responsive or would the passenger consider it invasive and post his negative experience on Facebook where other potential customers can see it?

• What if you walked into a retail store and the sales associate (having access to your shopping history from his Google Glass device) asked you if you would be interested in a tie to match the suit you bought the previous week? Would you find that incredibly responsive or would you find it creepy and never buy at that store again? How would immediate data access affect your relationship with the brand?

Still open to your consideration is that no single CRM application has all the answers. Success in any initiative must include a strong, documented, and tested understanding of the business processes and practices that make your company successful, independent from the technology. CRM strategy and technology go hand-in-hand. If you commit to nurturing your relationships, and manage the right interactions, you will be successful in both CRM strategy and technology deployment.

A number of factors will skew or sharpen your perception of what CRM technology is and how it applies to your company. Before you dismiss CRM technology based on what you read online or hear from the IT community, take time to evaluate and research the facts. Have an open mind and exercise fair judgment of what your company is doing with it.

The 2006 Forrester study referenced in Article 3 of this book also discusses best practices for ensuring the successful implementation of CRM solutions. These include:

- Defining data requirements and data quality approaches early

- Fostering user adoption

- Placing a high priority on software usability

- Simplifying the CRM platform

- Actively managing the vendor/partner relationship

We are the fortunate recipients of the gift of the internet and its unlimited access to feedback from people willing to give it. Today a person can type (or speak) a statement such as "CRM challenges in the retail industry" into a search engine and gain immediate access to the thoughts of millions of people. Use that information to understand what is heading your way and how others in your position worked through specific challenges to making CRM technology implementation a success.

CHANGE IS HERE

Chinese philosopher Lao Tzu said, "If you do not change direction, you may end up where you are heading." This is advice fitting to the state of CRM technology and the need to change how we manage customer relationship communications and experiences. Industry researchers are using terms like "imminent" and "disruptive" to describe the technologies that are changing CRM application and use. Imminent, because many of these changes are looming close by and are unstoppable stages in our technology evolution. Disruptive, because many of these changes are already here and forcing you to make business investments necessary to stay competitive. These technologies also disrupt the linear processes we have used for years to manage sales, marketing, and service interactions. They allow the customer to learn about you, make purchase decisions, get help, compare options, and buy on their terms and outside what we once knew as the linear customer lifecycle. In the new customer lifecycle, the experience does not begin when the customer buys. It happens every time the customer has a need and technology allows them to begin that cycle in many more places, with a lot more tools. Social and cultural changes in our customer's lives are forcing us to keep up.

When Gartner analysts delivered their keynote "The Nexus of Forces Changes Everything" at the Gartner Symposium/ITxpo 2012, it stimulated us to acknowledge collectively that we had to make significant changes to the current state of CRM technology. Do a search on CRM and you will find dozens of articles on how innovations in social media, the acceptance of cloud hosting, the dependency and commonplace use of mobile devices, and the ability to interpret and use data is changing our world. Gartner calls these "converging and mutually reinforcing social, cultural, and technological factors" the "Nexus of Forces."

IDC calls it the "Third Platform."

The CRM software we remember installing in user machines is gone; replaced by solutions on a service cloud. From there vendors keep it updated and companies manage software and upgrades simultaneously for all users. Users leverage their devices to access information from anywhere, including their technology-enabled vehicles. Marketing can now access data and make decisions not just based on responses to campaigns and advertisement, but on sentiment, feedback and live customer intelligence and interactions as they are happening in social media circles.

What we are seeing, is not as much a change in CRM but a growth in the capabilities and channels CRM uses to build relationships and improve the customer experience. The cloud is a more efficient way to manage software solutions and data and centrally manage the business processes that run your business. Mobility is an innovative portable means to access information you can use to learn more about the customer and make better decisions about how to serve them. It is something Delta Airlines realized and put into action by outfitted its more than 19,000 flight attendants with mobile devices in an effort to improve customer service and facilitate on-board transactions. Social media is yet another channel where we interact with our customers. Social media allows people to meet and talk regardless of where they physically live and work; a limitation they also expect you to remove by listening, acting, engaging, and responding to social media conversations.

Social, mobility, advanced analytics, and cloud improvements do not do away with CRM. They improve and enhance it. They further enable it to do what it is intended to do. Changing its name to Cloud CRM or Social CRM only serves as a descriptive appendage that tells you that the technology vendor is staying up with the technological, social, and cultural changes. Social CRM is not a new type of CRM. It is CRM that includes the newest way people communicate, and meet, and learn about your company. Eventually, saying CRM is Social will be as redundant as calling the Internet the World Wide Web. The internet certainly is world-wide, but doesn't everyone understand that?

ARTICLE 9

POWER TO THE VERTICAL

WE WILL IMPROVE CRM BY
CONTINUOUSLY INCORPORATING
THE BUSINESS PROCESSES
THAT MAKE OUR INDUSTRY
SUCCESSFUL; CONSTANTLY ALERT
TO BEST PRACTICES ACROSS
OTHER INDUSTRIES.

cus·tom·ize transitive verb \ˈkəs-tə-ˌmīz\:to build, fit, or alter according to individual specifications[22]

"Pleasure in the job puts perfection in the work." - Aristotle

If CRM technology is part of your strategy to serve customers and strengthen your customer relationships, then it is also important you consider the investment of making each CRM solution relevant to how you do business and the requirements of your industry. We measure the success of CRM initiatives based on the customer's perception, and we measure the success of CRM based on the approval of the people who will use it. Adoption is dependent on the alignment of CRM function with the business processes an industry uses to meet the needs of customers and remain compliant with regulatory requirements. Many of the CRM tools available as customer relationship management applications can serve as an excellent starting point but may require additional customization to make it applicable to your industry.

The insurance industry is a great example. Insurance providers have products and services to sell. They have sales, marketing, and support organizations that help them. They have business processes that add structure to the way they do business. You could implement one of the many commercial CRM solution available and could (after adding some customer data) almost immediately manage contact and account records, schedule activities, assign resources, manage sales pipeline, and create customer service tickets.

However, to use the CRM application to sell insurance, you need the system to support the insurance business. If it cannot do that, then it is not of any good to anyone. In fact, it could potentially slow you down. What will make this CRM solution effective is its ability to facilitate business through the animation and arbitration of the processes determined sufficient for insurance businesses. CRM can manage campaigns, but insurance companies need those campaigns to control how people receive them, who they are, and how they will register for educational events that help them make a decision about the insurance they need. CRM can manage appointment scheduling, but insurance companies need adequately to assign agents best trained and certified to sell certain products. CRM can store documents like applications and eligibility forms, but insurance companies need a system that can manage the paramount "started but not completed" application and help get the customer to finish the process.

CRM must be about the way the insurance company does business and support processes like the proactive review of the customer's first bill, new policy processing, up-sell and cross-sell, first notice of loss, orphaned policy holder assignment, and hundreds of other insurance-specific processes.

Some years back, while trying to explain the benefits of leveraging a commercially available CRM software solution to expedite the development CRM software for a state government agency, I compared the process to the way a car racing company may use a Formula One chassis to expedite creating a new, more powerful, race car. This is a common practice in that industry that saves hundreds of thousands of dollars through the repurposing of car parts. The investment required to build a brand new car is high and wrecking a new racecar is just heartbreaking after you have spent so much time and money to build it from nothing. By leveraging an existing chassis as the foundation, racecar companies directly benefit from the frame and basic functional machineries that make the car drivable and focus their investment on building the components specific to their race.

Doing the same thing with CRM technology yields similar benefits to you as you implement CRM technology appropriate to the needs of your industry. Using existing CRM technology allows you to assess your needs and align them with what the CRM application already has as a foundation. You can then use a solution that may already include forty to fifty percent of what you need and quickly adapt elements such as screens, forms, dashboards, reports and similar attributes to meet your requisites.

Even though there are similarities across sales, marketing,

and support regardless of the product or service you sell, there will be changes to the interface and nomenclature of an out-of-the-box CRM solution that go beyond the basic "face-lift" (minimal changes to field labels, field location, etc.). These are details relevant specifically to your industry and sub-specialties within that industry. The extent of the changes will vary from one industry to the next and could be as simple as changing certain naming conventions (such as from "contact" to "client" or "constituent") or as complicated as changing the solution to fit the various processes that run your business. In any case, these changes must always reflect the way you will use and navigate what will become "your" Formula One racecar.

The extent of the changes will vary by industry and may not always be obvious. Financial Services firms may need customer information to be arranged based on client status. Pharmaceutical sales reps that travel a lot from one physician's office to another may need fields arranged in a way that makes it easy to enter data while they are on the road. Law firms may need to simplify general information screens to make it easier for attorneys to share their Rolodex with the rest of the firm and later find contact information readily in the database of firm clients. How you need to see and access information will determine the changes you make.

There are many industry-specific online forums where you can interact with people ready to share their experiences. Such is the case with a recent online forum for automotive dealerships that illustrate this point very well. The site was created specifically for car dealers as a forum to determine the best type of automotive CRM solutions. The forum, while open to the public, warns vendors not to "spam the thread" with comments about how their CRM solution fits perfectly into the dealer management world. With the clear "don't give us your vision" message to vendors in place, the forum opens the door for dealers to express their needs and the value they would get from specific features in a CRM solution. Because the forum is open to customers wanting to provide feedback about their car-buying experience, the feedback includes a very useful and unbiased view of what CRM in this industry should accomplish for both the auto dealers and the consumer.

MORE THAN A FACE-LIFT

For a CRM system to work within an industry, it must first fit your culture. Financial advisors, accountants, lawyers, architects, and entertainment agents all have their own way of conducting business within their trade. These cultural nuances and behaviors must be integrated into the functionality of the CRM application, or it will be more difficult (sometimes impossible) for you to use it and make it applicable to the way you interact with your customers. In some cases, you may find a vendor that has made an investment in your industry and may have already gapped those cultural differences and deliver a product recognized and customized for your market. When that is not the case, and you have to take on these adaptations and customizations on your own, you will need to consider some things. The next few pages will help you determine if an industry-specific solution is the best fit, or if you should use a foundation solution and build from there.

WHO IS YOUR CUSTOMER?

Clients, constituents, franchisees, patients: companies have different names for their customers. Those customers could be individual consumers or companies, or both. Many CRM solutions start as an account-centric (company-centric) tool, which is very different from a contact management solution (that stores contact data without associating the people that work for the same company). While the account-centric approach is advantageous for most companies, it presents a challenge for others.

Consider that in a business environment where the "customer" could be either a company or person, a company-centric system will require that you define how information will be organized to best fit the way you do business. The concepts behind "account management" and "primary contact relationships" may need to be redefined to accommodate this dynamic. Carefully assess the dynamic of your customer's customers (and do not forget their partners and suppliers). It is common for a solution to easily accommodate a business with consumers, but not a model like that of a franchise in which your franchise owners are your customers, but your franchises have customers (end customers,) which you also need to account for in the CRM system.

PRODUCTS OR SERVICES?

It is a grave error to approach the sales cycle and opportunity management process of any organization strictly based on the existing model of the CRM technology you are buying. Opportunity management modules available in most CRM tools are an excellent foundation and powerful for companies that follow a conventional sales cycle that progresses from lead generation to product sale, and ultimately to service and support. In this model, a product is priced (sometimes configured), then quoted, then invoiced, and finally turned over for a support organization to support. This is not always the model companies follow, and not at all the pattern for organizations that sell a service.

For companies that sell services, estimating the value of an opportunity is calculated in ways not always supported (and often considered "non-traditional") by many CRM systems. Companies that sell services and have to manage people, time, and projects in CRM may find it challenging to use existing CRM solutions without adding solutions and plugins that extend CRM's functionality. Expect some integration to other business-essential data that may be stored in litigation, point-of-sales, point-of-service, or e-commerce systems. This is an area where vendors that offer "all-in-one" solutions have an enormous advantage and may offer the best value. Assessing the ROI of building utilities and tools that take CRM the rest of the way you need it to go must weigh heavily on your decision to select the right CRM tool.

ARTICLE 10

POWER TO THE ENDEAVOR

WE WILL TAKE NOTICE THAT CRM IS AN ENDEAVOR TO IMPROVE THE LIVES OF OUR CUSTOMERS, EMPLOYEES, AND OUR BUSINESS.

```
en·deav·or verb \in-ˈde-vər\ : to
seriously or continually try to do
(something)²³
```

"Perseverance is failing 19 times and succeeding the 20th." - Julie Andrews

The sad tale of the meeting shared at the beginning of this book is a real story. The company referenced is no longer in business. The people in that conference room did not part ways amicably, and they did not leave the experience behind as "just business." Real people were hurt emotionally and financially as the result of that event. The customer lost their trust in the CRM process and the project team, and the CRM corporate sponsor lost her job. The most tragic part of this story is that there was a tremendous opportunity to use this experience to learn to collaborate in other aspects of the business; a core problem that attributed to the eventual demise of the company.

TOYS NOT INCLUDED

A while back I was asked what I thought was the toughest challenge to overcome when introducing CRM to a company. I thought for a moment about things like value proposition and convincing sales people to share their contacts. After seriously thinking about it, I am compelled to answer that the toughest conversation I have with my customers is around the impact of CRM across their business. While ROI and CRM tool-selection and deployment are usually the first topics to emerge, discussing the idea that CRM is for everyone in the company (not just sales, or marketing or customer service) has always been the most challenging to address. That's because, to many customers, the idea of everyone having access to CRM translates to paying for more licenses or including additional stakeholders who may not be completely on board with the concept. Both of these objections immediately reveal that many companies either see CRM as "the tool" or the "thing" sales uses to manage customers.

Engaging in the "company-wide CRM" conversation makes business sense. It forces people to think about CRM as a strategic initiative; one that carefully orchestrates plans and methods for winning and retaining customer. CRM is more than the tool we use to manage the customer lifecycle. It is a vehicle to connect all the people in your company with the vision of improving the central relationships of your business through meaningful interactions. When you define it that way, CRM must be used by everyone who contributes to the customer relationship; even if the CRM tool itself is deployed in phases.

Approaching CRM as the exclusive project of a single

organization (usually sales, marketing, or support) is common. A sales or support organization, for example, (at law firms it is usually marketing) may sell their corporate sponsor on the need to implement CRM independently and thereby secure funding for the project. I am not finding fault in that. In a tight economy, it is easier to get funding for CRM for one function and then progressively bring in other organizations (maybe even have each organization fund their own effort). That approach resembles buying a set of batteries for your kids for Christmas with a note on it that says, "toys not included" (from one of my favorite Bernard Manning quotes). The root cause is failure to sell corporate sponsors on the value of CRM as a company-wide initiative that deploys a common CRM vision and technology strategy to support every organization.

So, think "corporate" initiative from the beginning. Do not neglect the strategy conversation that paints the picture of what CRM will mean to everyone. Get consensus even if every group isn't ready or does not have a budget for a company-wide implementation. If you are not ready to have that conversation but must implement a solution, then stay away from talking about CRM and address the project as a sales force automation, marketing automation, or support / case management automation initiative. I have heard people use the term "we can just turn that component or feature off" to placate to managers who do not see the need for the other components of CRM. That is a mistake. Always address the need for CRM as a company-wide need.

If you find it difficult to engage at the functional level (sales, marketing, and support), direct the dialog towards the core building blocks of the business. Talk about the customer segments and value proposition you offer customers in an effort to win and retain them. Talk about the channels, activities, and key resources that influence revenue stream and cost structure. The conversation will soon lead to the various groups that must be involved in making CRM implementation a success. Incidentally, this approach also allows you to address customer needs for social media, mobility, analytics, and hosting. Using this approach, you will gain company-wide collaboration and commitment for CRM.

BUILDING THE RELATIONSHIPS THAT BUILD YOUR BUSINESS

My eight-year-old daughter Addie is truly her father's daughter. When I tell people what I do and she is close enough to hear the conversation, she precariously follows my introduction of the term "CRM" with, "that means Customer Relationship Management." That is amazing to me because of a couple of curious facts: First she is only eight. Second, many of my own customers get the acronym wrong. What amazes me most about Addie's understanding of my job is that, despite her finite grasp of what CRM is, she knows that her daddy helps people with their relationships.

Throughout my career, I have worked for CRM software vendors several times. This is, in fact, how I started my career in CRM. But as I began to work through partner channels, and our attention was more focused on industry solutions (and I emphasize solutions because that is what they are; not accelerators), my focus began to shift away from the technology and steadily towards the people my customers where serving. Not just towards their customers, but towards all the people who help win and keep customers feeling rewarded for doing business with them. The guiding principal slowly overpowered the "relational" mentality of connected tables and metadata that CRM is about relationships.

After so many years working on the technology side of CRM it is easy to let your mind go to the technology. We have to change our mindset to thinking about the result rather than the tools you use to get there. The classic "Marketing Myopia" 1960 article quote by Theodore Levitt, "People don't buy quarter inch drills, they buy quarter inch holes" is equally applicable to CRM technology. People are not buying a CRM tool, they are buying a means to stronger customer relationships and customer experiences. They are buying customer knowledge and (dare I say it), customer intimacy. Technologist and CRM system implementers should never lose sight of that. Just as a fire extinguisher manufacturer knows they are in the business of fighting fires, and pharmaceutical companies know their mandate is to heal people and give them a better standard of living, we should be about the business of helping people build the relationships that make their business. We may not build businesses, but we build the relationships that build them.

No effort is more worthy than that which improves the quality of the life of another. No effort deserves more respect that the endeavor of engaging another human being for the purpose of being of service to them. It is easy to become overwhelmed by the daily toil of work and the sometimes unreasonable expectations of people outside and inside our company. It makes it easy to forget that the business processes we follow are not there just to help us win business. They are there to guide us through the process of building a relationship or to assess the level of interaction we should have with someone in order to guide that relationship.

When sales people reach out to a prospect, it is easy to allow sales quota to drive behavior (especially at the end of the quarter). But salespeople are not just selling, they are providing solutions to problems and CRM helps them to focus on building relationships that make people feel that they are making the right decisions.

Marketing people have the difficult task educating customers about your brand. Market competition and the increase in consumer knowledge about you and your competitors make it hard for marketing people to use the right methods and effectively use marketing lists, campaigns, and product marketing strategies. CRM ensures that customers appropriately perceive their interactions with marketing as sincere efforts to educate and help. When CRM does not effectively help marketing, customers receive duplicate correspondence, unwanted calls, and existing customers are sold products and services they already have. And although customers at large know that this type of thing happens, deep down when they receive marketing that is misdirected or undermines their relationship with you, they really feel like you do not care about them or know them as you should.

When people do not get a certain level of empathy from customer service agents, they remember your lack of service and your failure to treat them as someone who should come first. Likewise, when Heather from Geico ends her call with me with "thank you for being our customer for the past 10 years" she is leveraging CRM to show that longevity in our relationship is something her company values.

A FINAL WORD OF ENCOURAGEMENT

The September 27 issue of the New York Times includes dozens of stories of veterans who cannot receive their pensions because of the lack of adequate customer relationship and customer experience processes and systems that could improve customer service operations. It tells the story of Doris Hink, the widow of a World War II veteran who had to wait nearly two years to process her claim for a survivor's pension, forcing her daughter to take $12,000 from savings to pay nursing home bills. A December 20, 2012 Daily Beast article reports that in the fiscal year that ended in September, the Department of Veteran Affairs paid $437 million in retroactive benefits to the survivors of nearly 19,500 veterans who died waiting.

The CRM endeavor is not simply a means to manage

information about people. It is a worthy endeavor that, when implemented successfully, can improve the lives of the people we serve. The CRM mandate is a call for each of you to acknowledge the value of a strategy that helps you be more accountable to the customers you serve as much as to the people who make customers feel rewarded for doing business with you. CRM is about people and building genuine relationships with them, and its benefits can truly help make a difference that can also affect your life in a positive way.

There are moments of exuberance and joy in my job when the faces of my customer's customer are people whose quality of life will improve because of this thing we call CRM. Of equal enjoyment are those moments when people "get it" and we celebrate together the successful completion of a CRM strategic or technology effort. Not because it is so rare to see CRM efforts succeed, but because I know that with the right focus, every CRM initiative can be a successful enterprise.

May this book be of enrichment to your business, and may you find in its pages something that changes your own life, as well, for the best.

I wish you the greatest of success.

SPECIAL ACKNOWLEDGEMENTS

MENTORS
Dr. Michael LeBoeuf for his professional and personal advice.

Dr. Dan Dana for introducing me to the value of workplace conflict management.

Pat Sullivan for introducing me to this business.

PARTNERS
John Marchica for trusting me as colleague.

Whit McIsaac for sharing his vision of building a trail-blazing vertical business and letting me be a part of it.

FRIENDS
Floyd Spencer for being there through the good and bad.

Chuck Ingram for his genuine friendship.

Gary Bell for encouraging me to finish this book.

Kevin Troy Darling for his contribution as editor and wordsmith over this work; thank you for never judging my many faults.

CUSTOMERS
"One is glad to be of service"

REFERENCES PAGE:

[1] Merriam-Webster Dictionary

[2] Merriam-Webster Dictionary

[3] Merriam-Webster Dictionary

[4] http://www.thekitchn.com/51-per-pound-the-deceptive-cost-of-single-serve-coffee-the-new-york-times-165712

[5] WEBER, Craig (2013). "Conversational Capacity: The Secret to Building Successful Teams That Perform When the Pressure Is On Merriam-Webster Dictionary". McGraw-Hill.

[6] RITTEL, Horst, WEBBER, Melvyn (1969). "Dilemmas in a General Theory of Planning. Panel on Policy Sciences, American Association for the Advancement of Science".

[7] FARREL, Michael (2003). "Collaborative Circles: Friendship Dynamics and Creative Work". Farrell. University of Chicago Press.

[8] PAINE, Christopher E.; COCHRAN, Thomas B.; NORRIS, Robert S. (1996). "The Arsenals of the Nuclear Weapons Powers: An Overview". Natural Resources Defense Council.

[9] MANNING, Harley; BODINE, Kerry; BERNOFF, Josh (2012). Outside In: The Power of Putting Customers at the Center of Your Business". New Harvest.

[10] Merriam-Webster Dictionary

[11] Merriam-Webster Dictionary

[12] SANDERS, Tm (2003). "Love Is the Killer App: How to Win Business and Influence Friends". Crown Business.

[13] LEVINGER, George; RAUSH, Harold (1977). Close Relationships: Perspectives on the Meaning of Intimacy".

[14] Merriam-Webster Dictionary

[15] SEARCY, Tom (2009). "RFPs Suck! How to Master the RFP System Once and for All to Win Big Business". Channel V Books

[16] DEGREGOR, Dennison (2010). "The Customer- Transparent Enterprise: How Market Leaders are Using 21st Century Customer Transparency to Close the Brand/Customer Gap and Win the Customer Loyalty Wars". Motivational Press.

[17] Merriam-Webster Dictionary

[18] LEBOEUF, Michael (2000). "How to Win Customers and Keep Them for Life". Berkley Trade.

[19] Merriam-Webster Dictionary

[20] ANDERSON, E. W.; FORNELL, C. (1994). "A customer satisfaction research prospective". In R.T. Rust & R. L. Oliver

[21] Merriam-Webster Dictionary

[22] Merriam-Webster Dictionary

[23] Merriam-Webster Dictionary

CPSIA information can be obtained at www.ICGtesting.com
Printed in the USA
LVOW12*0821130814

398728LV00006B/43/P